## A message from the author.

Thank you for reading this book.

Travel can be one of the great adventures of a lifetime. It can also be one of the most frustrating. The contributors wanted to share their experiences, both good and bad, so that your trip is filled with fun instead of frustration.

On your travels you may experience a special hotel, airline, cruise ship, restaurant, or other "find" you would like to share with our readers. Please drop us a note, email: jfeldman@doctor-travel.com or FAX 312-527-9112.

We welcome your comments, stories, and travel tips. Any contributor will be acknowledged in the book.

Doctor Travel will soon be publishing additional books that include:

- Travel Tips for Women Travelling Alone
- Travel Tips for Children Travelling With Adults
- Travel Tips for Travelling With Pets
- What To Do When You Are Stuck In An Airport

http://www.doctor-travel.com

# Doctor Travel's®
## Cure for the Common Trip

*"What to know before you go"*

*James Feldman*

Sage Creek Press

Traverse City, Michigan

Copyright © 1999 by James Feldman

*All rights reserved.* No part of this book may be reproduced or transmitted in any form or by any means, electronic or mechanical, including photocopying, recording or any information storage and retrieval system, without permission in writing from the author, except for the inclusion of brief quotations in a review.

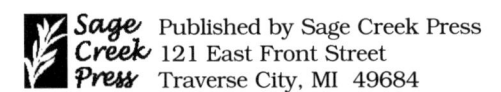

**Sage Creek Press**  Published by Sage Creek Press
121 East Front Street
Traverse City, MI 49684

Publisher's Cataloging-in-Publication Data
Feldman, James.
  Doctor Travel's Cure For The Common Trip : What To Know Before You Go / James Feldman – Chicago, IL:
Sage Creek Press, 1999.

          p.   ill.   cm.

  Includes bibliographical references.
  ISBN: 1-890394-30-0
  1. Travel I. Title. II. Doctor Travel's
Cure For The Common Trip.

G151  .F45  1999              98-87461
910.4 – dc21                  CIP

Cover Design and Illustrations by Michelle Hove
Project Coordination by Jenkins Group, Inc.

03  02  01  00  *  5  4  3  2  1

Printed in United States of America

Some information in this book was previously published under the name "Wing Tips." All rights to the book were purchased by James Feldman from the author, Allen Klein, MA, CSP.

## About the Author

James Feldman (a.k.a. Doctor Travel) started travelling with his parents at an early age. When Jim was only 18, he began his own travel company, called BreakAway Tours, for college students. In the 80s, Jim helped create the concept of individual incentive travel awards.

As president of Incentive Travelers Cheque International, Inc. and **Shift Happens!**®, he has a vast knowledge of how to anticipate, prevent, and handle travel problems. His travels, with such clients as Toyota, Apple, Xerox, Mary Kay, NBC, Lexus, Clairol, Neutrogena, Helene Curtis, and Compaq, have taken Jim around the world. Once Jim won two tickets to Milan, Italy, in a Pavarotti look-alike contest in Michigan. He donated the tickets to charity. As an international speaker and consultant, Jim has worked with hotel chains, airlines, and tourism development for such diverse locations as Puerto Rico, Australia, South Africa, Norway, Singapore, Hawaii, and Scotland.

Jim has planned and implemented trips for over a million travelers and he has traveled to dozens of countries, visited hundreds of cities, and flown millions of miles.

# Preface

This book's purpose is to help provide you with a trouble-free journey. This is not a book about where to go but, instead, it's a book about how to prepare for the adventure and how to deal with any problems that may occur.

Here are my own ten travel commandments:

1. Make your reservation early.
2. Get a seat assignment.
3. Request a special meal, even a kid's meal.
4. Ask for a reasonable amount of time between airplane connections.
5. Carry confirmation letters or numbers for hotel and car rentals.
6. Take only credit cards that have not reached their credit limit.
7. Familiarize yourself with your travel plans. Either leave a schedule at home or at your business so you can be contacted, if necessary.
8. Take any medications with you. Do not pack anything you may need on the trip.
9. Stretch, relax, chat, read, watch a movie, and drink only nonalcoholic liquids.
10. Ask for help!

Because I travel over 200 days a year, I see almost every type of delay, problem, or opportunity presented to the modern-day traveler. Through the years, I've talked with thousands of travelers who

Dr. Travel Prescribes:
Preface

have learned how to cope with the challenges that occur during their travels. Like me, they have "been there and done that." And like me, they are still learning the joyous part of travel is discovery.

Please send your comments, stories, suggestions, and travel tips to our Web site at http://www.doctor-travel.com.

*The world is a book and those who do
not travel read only a page.*
— St. Augustine

# Acknowledgments

Doctor Travel wants to thank the following people — without whom this book would have taken a different journey — for their contributions:

To my mother and father, who always wanted me to go somewhere . . . anywhere . . . as long as I took them along. My parents loved the concept of free travel, even if I was the one paying.

To Michelle Hove, whose cartoon creation of Doctor Travel visualized my concept and gave me the stimulus to put words on paper. Michelle shared her energy, support, and encouragement with me to complete the book, one chapter at a time. Her character is what recognized my character so accurately and, for this, I can never thank Michelle enough.

To Mindy Levine whose assistance in research, syntax, proof reading, and general sounding board provided me with the stimulus to continue this project, even when I did not want to continue. Call her, ask her to stop by, she bakes the best cheesecake brownies on the planet.

To Marcia Baker — my editor, wordsmith, and longtime friend — whose meticulous editing and careful attention to detail crafted this book into a coherent, concise finished product. My longest, most uphill battle was convincing Marcia I would deliver what I promised (when I promised it!) and not be too much of a Hertz to her.

To Rusty Citron, founder of As Seen On, a consummate entrepreneur and traveler. Rusty sees the world through the

## Dr. Travel Prescribes: Acknowledgments

eyes of a child, the wallet of a tycoon, and the family of his daughters, who have taught him the best adventure of all may be in his own backyard.

To Joseph Sugarman, a man who constantly reinvents himself. As founder of JS&A, Joe introduced the first pocket calculator and then developed BluBlocker Sunglasses, creating one of the most recognized brand names in the industry. Joe said, "Go, Jim! Go for your dreams! Go . . . anywhere! Just go away!" Without Joe's advice, I would still be there.

To Robert Baseman, former executive vice president of Encyclopedia Britannica, who taught me timing is everything. Bob got out of town just when the world discovered CD-ROMs were much smaller and lighter than 200 pounds of books. Bob and his wife, Gwen, taught me travel is twice as much fun, at any age, when two people travel together. Travel is meant to be shared; business trips are not.

To Dr. Alan Steen and his wife Charlene, who taught me that travel is for those who make time to go, save some cash, and enjoy a never ending desire to learn about the world. They are my favorite "frequent flyers."

And, finally, to my dear friend, the late Harry Blackstone, Jr., America's foremost magician. Harry told me " . . . be brief! Everyone loves to be mystified . . . but not fooled. Tell your stories, give them the facts, and send them on their way. Part of the magic of travel is solving the problems."

# Contents at a Glance

*Preface*      vii
*Acknowledgments*      ix

## Part I: Get Ready for Take-Off      1

### The Mental Preparation
Chapter 1:   Common Sense      5
Chapter 2:   A Sense of Humor      19
Chapter 3:   A Sense of Adventure      33

### The Physical Preparation
Chapter 4:   Choosing a Travel Agent      43
Chapter 5:   Choosing a Flight      47
Chapter 6:   Choosing a Seat      59
Chapter 7:   Cheap Travel      69
Chapter 8:   Cheaper Travel      79
Chapter 9:   Why Do You Think They Call It "Luggage?"      89
Chapter 10:  Wheels of Fortune      95
Chapter 11:  Special Travel Needs      109

## Part II: Off and Skipping      114
Chapter 12:  Get Me to the Airport on Time      115
Chapter 13:  All Airports Are Not Created Equal      121
Chapter 14:  To Check . . . or Not to Check . . . That Is the Question      129
Chapter 15:  The Zen of Flying      137

Dr. Travel Prescribes:
Contents at a Glance

| | | |
|---|---|---|
| **Part III: Up, Up, and Away** | | **146** |
| Chapter 16: | How To Be Comfortable While Being Confined | 147 |
| Chapter 17: | Let Me Entertain Me | 157 |
| Chapter 18: | Travel Broadens (or, You Are What You Eat) | 165 |
| Chapter 19: | Be Fit While You Sit | 171 |
| Chapter 20: | A Crash Course in Airline Safety | 177 |
| Chapter 21: | Jet Lag: Eat, Wash, or Smell It Away? | 187 |
| **Part IV: Upon Arrival** | | **195** |
| Chapter 22: | Renting a Car | 197 |
| Chapter 23: | Renting a Room | 201 |
| Chapter 24: | Son of Travel Broadens | 227 |
| Chapter 25: | Staying In Shape when You're Out of Town | 235 |
| Chapter 26: | Cruise Control for Auto-Pilots | 237 |
| **Part V: Returning Home** | | **244** |
| Chapter 27: | Home, Sweet Home | 245 |
| Epilogue: | Beyond the Blue Horizon | 247 |

# Contents

*Preface* vii
*Acknowledgments* ix

**Part I: Get Ready for Take-Off** 1

**The Mental Preparation**
Chapter 1: Common Sense 5
Common Sense from a Monkey 6
Right or Happy? 8
Common Sense from
 Mother Teresa 8
Common Sense from a Stranger 9
Common Sense from a Child 10
Common Sense Rules #1, 2, & 3 11
Be Nice to Airport Personnel 12
Common Sense Rule # 4 14
Common Sense Rule # 5 14
Common Sense Rule # 6 14
Common Sense Rule # 7 14
Common Sense Rule # 8 14
Common Sense Rule # 9 15
Common Sense Rule #10 15
Common Sense Rule #11 15
Common Sense Rule #12 16
Common Sense Rule #13 16
Things Could Be Worse 16
Keep Things in Perspective 17
Chapter 2: A Sense of Humor 19
Pack Perky Pick-Me-Ups 19

Dr. Travel Prescribes:
Contents

|  |  |  |
|---|---|---|
|  | Goofs Become Giggles | 20 |
|  | Wear Something Unusual | 21 |
|  | Pretend You're on *Totally Hidden Video* | 23 |
|  | Take a Lesson from the Flight Attendants | 23 |
|  | You Are Noble and You Should Be Rewarded | 24 |
|  | Northwest Orients Its Passengers | 25 |
|  | The Groaners of Today Are the Grins of Tomorrow | 26 |
|  | Go Ahead, Make Your Day | 28 |
|  | Letter from the United Pilot | 28 |
|  | Kids Say the Darndest Things | 29 |
|  | Increase Your Smileage | 30 |
|  | Jest for the Fun of It | 31 |
| Chapter 3: | A Sense of Adventure | 33 |
|  | Expect the Unexpected | 35 |
|  | Oh Goodie . . . Another Adventure! | 36 |
|  | Airline Red Carpet Treatment | 39 |
|  | *The Physical Preparation* | 41 |
| Chapter 4: | Choosing a Travel Agent | 43 |
|  | Why You Need a Travel Agent | 44 |
|  | How to Find a Good Travel Agent | 45 |
|  | Once You Find a Travel Agent | 46 |
|  | Become Your Own Agent | 46 |
| Chapter 5: | Choosing a Flight | 47 |
|  | Know Some Airline Lingo | 48 |
|  | Don't Set It Up for Failure | 50 |
|  | Take the First, Avoid the Last | 50 |
|  | Nonstop Flights . . . the Best? | 50 |
|  | Know Your Options | 51 |
|  | Call Again | 52 |
|  | Book Off-Peak Flights and Less-Used Airports | 53 |
|  | Know Your ABCs | 53 |
|  | Know Who's Late, Who's Not | 54 |

|  |  |  |
|---|---|---|
|  | Know the Rules | 54 |
|  | Know Your Plane | 56 |
|  | Something Special in the Air | 58 |
| Chapter 6: | Choosing a Seat | 59 |
|  | Aisle Seat | 60 |
|  | Window Seat | 61 |
|  | Front of Plane | 61 |
|  | Back of Plane | 62 |
|  | Get an Advanced Seat Assignment | 63 |
|  | Request an Exit Row | 63 |
|  | Request a Bulkhead Seat . . . Maybe | 64 |
|  | Lift the Armrest | 65 |
|  | When You "Vant to Be Alone" | 66 |
|  | When Only Middle Seats Remain | 67 |
|  | Upgrade Whenever You Can | 67 |
|  | Play Musical Chairs | 68 |
| Chapter 7: | Cheap Travel | 69 |
|  | The Weekend Stay-Over | 70 |
|  | The One-Stop | 70 |
|  | The Fare Wars | 71 |
|  | The Split | 72 |
|  | The Throw-Away | 72 |
|  | The Advance Purchase | 73 |
|  | The Double-Overlapping Open-Jaw | 73 |
|  | The Buy and Fly | 74 |
|  | The Unconventional | 75 |
|  | The Close-Enough | 75 |
|  | The Hidden City | 76 |
|  | The Special Fare | 76 |
|  | Fare Warning | 77 |
|  | *Best Fares* Magazine | 78 |
| Chapter 8: | Cheaper Travel | 79 |
|  | Consolidators | 79 |

Dr. Travel Prescribes:
Contents

|  |  |  |
|---|---|---|
|  | Get More Value by Not Using Your Frequent Flyer Miles to Obtain Your Ticket | 82 |
|  | Nonstop Way to Free Flights | 82 |
|  | Once You Join, Keep Track of Your Mileage | 83 |
|  | Bumping | 84 |
|  | If You Don't Want to Be Bumped | 85 |
|  | If You Want to Be Bumped | 85 |
|  | Before You Take the Ticket and Run | 85 |
|  | The Start-Ups | 86 |
|  | Courier Travel | 86 |
|  | No Matter What You Pay | 87 |
| Chapter 9: | Why Do You Think They Call It "Luggage?" | 89 |
|  | Making a Case for the Suitcase | 89 |
|  | Making a Case for Luggage Carts | 91 |
|  | Become a Member of the Tag Team | 92 |
|  | For Safety's Sake | 92 |
|  | Some Packing Tips | 93 |
| Chapter 10: | Wheels of Fortune | 95 |
|  | Tote Bags | 97 |
|  | Gym Bags | 97 |
|  | Single Purpose Bags | 98 |
|  | Overnight Bags | 98 |
|  | Bags You Use for a Business Trip | 98 |
|  | Before You Buy Luggage . . . | 99 |
|  | Bags You Take on Vacation | 102 |
|  | Travel Kit/Cosmetic Pouch | 104 |
|  | Passport/Ticket Holder | 104 |
|  | A Few Packing Tips | 105 |
| Chapter 11: | Special Travel Needs | 109 |
|  | Suggestions for Seniors | 109 |
|  | Have Handicap, Will Travel | 110 |
|  | Trekking with Tykes | 111 |

| | | |
|---|---|---|
| **PART II: Off and Skipping** | | **114** |
| Chapter 12: | Get Me to the Airport on Time | 115 |
| | Beat the Clock . . . Not! | 115 |
| | Before You Go | 116 |
| | Car, Cab or Coach? | 116 |
| | Consider the Options | 118 |
| | Make It a Repeat Performance | 118 |
| Chapter 13: | All Airports Are Not Created Equal | 121 |
| | Amuse Yourself | 121 |
| | Catch Up on Culture | 122 |
| | Invest Your Time | 123 |
| | Keeping Kids Content | 123 |
| | Looking Good | 123 |
| | Pray Away a Flight Delay | 124 |
| | Read All About It | 124 |
| | Shop 'til You Drop | 124 |
| | Smell the Flowers | 125 |
| | Win Some, Lose Some | 125 |
| | Work It Out | 125 |
| | Getting Your Zs | 125 |
| | Hey, Look Me Over | 126 |
| | Far from the Madding Crowd | 126 |
| | Familiarity Breeds Comfort | 127 |
| Chapter 14: | To Check . . . or Not to Check . . . That Is the Question | 129 |
| | On a Long Journey Even a Straw Weighs Heavy | 130 |
| | To Check | 130 |
| | . . . or Not to Check | 131 |
| | Never Check | 131 |
| | If You Check | 132 |
| | Ninety-eight Percent of Lost Bags Are Returned | 134 |
| | If Your Bags Go Astray | 134 |
| | If You Carry on | 135 |
| Chapter 15: | The Zen of Flying | 137 |

Dr. Travel Prescribes:
Contents

|  | Be Here Now | 137 |
|---|---|---|
|  | Take a Deep Breath | 138 |
|  | Create Your Own Airport Ritual | 139 |
|  | Remember It's a Process | 140 |
|  | When One Door Closes, Another Opens | 140 |
|  | Physical Opportunities | 141 |
|  | Inner Growth Opportunities | 143 |
|  | Be a Winner | 145 |
| **PART III:** | **Up, Up, and Away** | **146** |
| Chapter 16: | How to Be Comfortable While Being Confined | 147 |
|  | Grab a Pillow | 147 |
|  | Take Slumber Gear | 148 |
|  | Wear Loose Fitting Clothing (or None?) | 148 |
|  | Change Your Position | 149 |
|  | Travel and Be Well | 149 |
|  | Become a Portable Drugstore | 150 |
|  | High and Dry | 150 |
|  | Flood Yourself with Fluids | 151 |
|  | When You Don't Fly First Class | 152 |
|  | Customer Satisfaction | 153 |
|  | Why Doesn't My Connecting Flight Ever Leave from the Gate Next to Where I Landed? | 154 |
|  | Why Are My Bags the Last to Arrive at the Baggage Claim? | 154 |
|  | Why Do Airlines Assign Middle Seats or Seats Next to a Crying Child, Especially When I Book Early? | 154 |
| Chapter 17: | Let Me Entertain Me | 157 |
|  | Carry on Reading Material | 157 |
|  | Plane Mail | 158 |
|  | Use the Headphones | 158 |

|  |  |  |
|---|---|---|
|  | Use Your Own Cassette or CD-ROM Player | 159 |
|  | Work | 159 |
|  | Play | 159 |
|  | Busy Be, Happy Be | 160 |
|  | People Watch | 160 |
|  | Reach Out and Meet Someone | 161 |
|  | Silencing Seatmates | 162 |
|  | Contemplate | 163 |
|  | Sleep | 164 |
| Chapter 18: | Travel Broadens (or, You Are What You Eat) | 165 |
|  | Eat Before You Board | 166 |
|  | Check the Meal Service | 166 |
|  | Take Your Own Food | 166 |
|  | Order a Special Meal | 167 |
|  | Drink to Your Health | 168 |
|  | Don't Eat the Nuts | 169 |
|  | First Class Meals | 169 |
|  | Don't Eat, Period | 170 |
| Chapter 19: | Be Fit While You Sit | 171 |
|  | Tense and Relax | 172 |
|  | Incorporate Some Isometrics | 172 |
|  | Let 'er Roll | 172 |
|  | Stretch It Out | 173 |
|  | Get Out of Your Seat | 174 |
|  | Get Exercise Rubber Bands | 175 |
| Chapter 20: | A Crash Course in Airline Safety | 177 |
|  | Easing the Fear | 179 |
|  | Increase Your Survival Odds | 182 |
|  | Stay Alert, Dress Properly, Know the Location of the Nearest Exit | 185 |
| Chapter 21: | Jet Lag: Eat, Wash, or Smell It Away? | 187 |
|  | What Is Jet Lag? | 187 |
|  | Sleep-Away Jet Lag | 189 |

|  |  |  |
|---|---|---|
|  | Change-Your-Watch Cure | 189 |
|  | Pop-a-Pill Cure | 189 |
|  | Supplement-Away Jet Lag | 190 |
|  | Eat-Away Jet Lag | 191 |
|  | Don't Eat Cure | 191 |
|  | Let-There-Be-Light Cure | 191 |
|  | Exercise-Away Jet Lag | 192 |
|  | Wash-Away Jet Lag | 192 |
|  | Smell-Away Jet Lag | 193 |
|  | Think-Away Jet Lag | 193 |
| **PART IV: Upon Arrival** |  | **195** |
| Chapter 22: | Renting a Car | 197 |
|  | When You Need Wheels | 197 |
| Chapter 23: | Renting a Room | 201 |
|  | Leisure versus Business | 206 |
|  | Keeping Comfort Up | 207 |
|  | Keeping Costs Down | 210 |
|  | Special Combination Offers | 220 |
|  | Check-In and Check-Out Times | 220 |
|  | Early Departure Penalties | 221 |
|  | Broadway Plays | 221 |
|  | Keeping Safe | 221 |
|  | Becoming a Hotel VIP | 223 |
| Chapter 24: | Son of Travel Broadens | 227 |
|  | Finding Good Eats | 228 |
|  | Make Meals Memorable | 228 |
|  | Feast for Less | 229 |
|  | Eat Healthy | 229 |
| Chapter 25: | Staying In Shape When You're Out of Town | 235 |
|  | I-Hate-to-Exercise Exercises | 235 |
| Chapter 26: | Cruise Control for Auto-Pilots | 237 |
|  | Muddied Waters Can Be Cleared | 238 |
|  | Daze versus Nights | 240 |
| **PART V: Returning Home** |  | **244** |
| Chapter 27: | Home, Sweet Home | 245 |
| Epilogue: | Beyond the Blue Horizon | 247 |

# 1

# Get Ready For Take-Off

*In the long run, the pessimist may be proved right, but the optimist has a better time on the trip.*
— Daniel L. Reardon

Part I:
Get Ready for Take-Off

> *The famous inventor Thomas Edison concluded, "It is apparent to me that the possibilities of the aeroplane... have been exhausted and that we must turn elsewhere."*
>
> *Wilbur Wright told his brother in 1901, just two years before the famous flight at Kitty Hawk, "Man will not fly for 50 years."*
>
> *In 1932, Boeing's 247 made its first flight. A company engineer triumphantly declared, "There will never be a bigger plane built."*
>
> So much for the experts.

"**\*\*!!##!!\*!!!\*\*####!!#\*\*##\*\*\*!!!\*!**" These expletives (sorry, folks — the actual words are unfit for family reading) are what many people utter when they encounter airline adversity.

Admittedly, good reasons may exist to curse the crowded skies, but getting upset about the trials and tribulations of air travel doesn't get you far, unless you're in the market for a massive coronary. Spending time and energy trying to fight a battle you have no chance of winning is simply unproductive.

On the other hand, you can **TAKE MENTAL CONTROL** of uncontrollable situations by using your three senses:

- common sense
- sense of humor
- sense of adventure

Using your three senses makes much more sense than **\*\*!!##!!\*!!!\*\*\*##\*#!!\*\*\*!!!\*!** if you want to be a stress-resistant, happier airline passenger. So don't leave home without them.

2

Part I:
Get Ready for Take-Off

Here is my blueprint — in chronological order — for any trip longer than five nights.

## Two Months Before the Trip:

- ☐ Plan a budget and itinerary
- ☐ Apply for passport and/or visa
- ☐ Purchase maps and guide books
- ☐ Get recommendations from friends and relatives for restaurants, hotels, and sightseeing
- ☐ Make reservations for airlines, hotels, rental cars, trains, and so forth
- ☐ Contact a travel agent, if necessary
- ☐ Check expiration dates on credit cards
- ☐ Have medical and dental checkups
- ☐ Get vaccinations
- ☐ Refill all medical prescriptions
- ☐ Get copies of all prescriptions, including eyeglasses
- ☐ Obtain emergency medical ID bracelets or cards
- ☐ Make arrangements for pet care

## One Month Before the Trip:

- ☐ Pay all monthly obligations in advance
- ☐ Arrange for a house-sitter
- ☐ Plan to have mail delivery put on hold or picked up by someone
- ☐ Arrange for lawn and garden care

## Two Weeks Before the Trip:

- ☐ Notify neighbors, relatives, and police of travel plans
- ☐ Cancel all regular deliveries
- ☐ Install automatic timers for lights and stereo
- ☐ Leave itinerary and key with trusted neighbor or relative
- ☐ Obtain phone numbers of the American Embassy and the American Consulate in the countries you will visit

Part I:
Get Ready for Take-Off

## One Week Before the Trip:

- ☐ Organize tickets, driver's license, passport, and credit cards in one zipper case
- ☐ Confirm all reservations and seat assignments
- ☐ Confirm you will get credit to your Frequent Flyers account
- ☐ Visit your bank to obtain foreign currency and Traveler's Cheques
- ☐ Put all valuables in safe deposit box
- ☐ Buy voltage converter and computer telephone plugs with adapters for all countries you will visit
- ☐ Buy twice as much film or video tape as you think you need
- ☐ Buy a new battery (and a spare) for your camera
- ☐ Make a list of any requests for gifts or purchases

## Just Before You Leave:

- ☐ Empty the refrigerator
- ☐ Check weather at your destination
- ☐ Turn off hot water
- ☐ Change answering machine. Indicate you will check messages, but you cannot return calls due to a personal commitment
- ☐ Turn down thermostat
- ☐ Check tickets, passports, and credit cards one last time
- ☐ Check to make certain all locks are securely closed
- ☐ Take pet to relatives, friend, or vet

*Simply put, you believe things or people make you unhappy, but this is not accurate. You make yourself unhappy.*

— Wayne Dyer

# Chapter 1
# Common Sense

An ancient proverb says: "The happiest people don't necessarily have the best of everything. They simply know how to make the best of everything." The first common sense concept for making the best of an ugly airline situation is to accept what you cannot change.

So your flight is delayed, you missed your connection, and on top of that your luggage is in Chicago and you are in Sheboygen.

The more you resist what has happened, the more unhappy you become. Instead of dwelling on the negative, accept what has happened. Look for what is right about the situation and move on.

"Acceptance," say John-Roger and Peter McWilliams in their wonderful book, *Life 101,* "is such an important commodity some have called it 'the first law of personal growth.' When you accept, you relax; let go; you become patient."

In other words, once you accept your circumstance, you move to a higher plane. Or, when you fly, to another plane. Often your circumstances will not change until you make the first move. Consider another airline. Consider another method of transportation or, if possible, consider another day. Many frequent travelers have told me stories of how they "felt something was wrong" when circumstances continued to delay their travel plans. So, if you don't feel right, make the effort to take charge of the situation.

Part I:
Get Ready for Take-Off

## Common Sense from a Monkey

Once, a monkey, who was searching for something to eat, put his hand in a trap containing food. The monkey was caught. What the monkey didn't realize was all he had to do to get out was to open his hand, release the food, and he would be freed from this predicament.

I have seen otherwise civilized people act as if they were wild monkeys when their flights were canceled or delayed or when their luggage was lost.

A little common sense, however, will tell you that you cannot battle the trials and tribulations of air travel with a clenched fist. In fact, the harder you tense, the more stress you create. You cannot yell at a ticket attendant, flight steward, or fellow passenger. It's a losing battle. The trick, which the monkey didn't learn — but you can learn — is to let go and stop struggling.

No matter which airline you fly, you can be sure of one thing. You will, at one time or another, experience delays, cancellations and, yes, missed connections. The airlines even publish a listing each month of which airline is the Queen of Delays. They know not every plane will depart or arrive on time. It's part of the turf (or should I say tarmac?). For your most recent copy, look for the report in *USA Today*, which offers the report each month in its travel section.

*The really happy man is one who can enjoy the scenery on a detour.*
— Anonymous

Common sense is to realize, if you are going to fly, you may get caught up in some of these problems. Yet many flyers forget this when they prepare for a trip.

Chapter 1
Dr. Travel Prescribes: Common Sense

In his book, *It Can't Happen to Me: 99 of Life's Most Distressing Problems,* author Samuel H. Klarreich writes that sometimes problems seem overwhelming. Klarreich reminds us we can master great difficulties by the powerful forces of the mind and we can refuse to give in to destructive thinking.

The challenge, Klarreich states, is to take unproductive thinking and replace it with a more constructive mental outlook. **Positive Mental Attitude (PMA)** is one of the most highly regarded cure-alls. Doctors report terminal illness can be arrested, people who were told they could not walk again determined to do otherwise. If they can do it, why can't you? Normal people have the ability to take control of their lives, no matter what the situation.

In other words, let go of your gloomy thoughts about the horrors of airline travel and turn them around. The next time you take a trip, tell yourself "No matter what happens (rude seat partners, noisy kids, whatever) I will stay in a good mood" or "I may not be in control of flight schedules, but I am in control of my own happiness."

Because you can frequently do nothing about the situation, try to let go of your anger and redirect your energy and focus on something positive. If you don't, you will be trapped like the monkey.

7

Part I:
Get Ready for Take-Off

# Travel Secret: Right or Happy?

The next time you get into an airline upset, ask yourself: Do I want to be right or do I want to be happy?

## Common Sense from Mother Teresa

"One day, after my conversation had been filled with a litany of problems," writes Eileen Egan, in her book, *Such a Vision of the Street*, Mother Teresa remarked, 'Everything is a problem. Why not use the word *gift*?' With that she began a shift in vocabulary.

"Shortly thereafter, we were to fly from Vancouver to New York City. I was dismayed to learn that the trip had to be broken en route, with a long delay, and was about to inform her of the problem. Then I caught myself and said, 'Mother, I have to tell you about a gift. We have to wait four hours here, and you won't arrive at the convent until very late.' Mother Teresa settled down in the airport to read a book of meditations, a favorite of hers.

"From that time on, items that presented disappointments or difficulties would be introduced with 'We have a small gift here' or 'Today we have an especially big gift.' There were smiles, perhaps rueful, at situations that earlier had been described by the dour word *problem*."

Anyone familiar with air travel knows that it can overflow with especially "big gifts." Can you turn your passenger problems into gifts?

# Chapter 1
## Dr. Travel Prescribes: Common Sense

> *Children have a remarkable talent for not treating the adult world with the kind of respect we are so confident it ought to be given... They refuse to appreciate the gravity of our monumental concerns, while we forget that if we were to become more like children our concerns might not be so monumental.*
> — Conrad Hyers

### Common Sense from a Stranger

One day I shared a taxi into town with a man who obviously knew how to turn problems into gifts. His flight was delayed for at least four hours so, instead of waiting around the airport and having a not-so-great meal there, he headed for the city to dine at a delightful little restaurant he knew.

Several months after meeting him, my 6:30 A.M. flight from my home city was canceled just before boarding. I started to wait the three-and-a-half hour delay when I remembered the man in the cab. I realized I could book a later flight and easily return to my office to get some work done or even take a nap.

Realizing you needn't wait around the airport if you have a long delay may seem like common sense. Yet many times flyers forget this option. The Singapore Tourist Board now offers a free tour of the city from the airport. Here is an extraordinary example of how to use downtime. The passenger can see sights of a country he or she may wish to revisit in the future at no risk. This is the best of both worlds, which is why the tourist board created this wonderful opportunity to showcase their city.

> *Life is a tragedy when seen in close-up, but a comedy in a long shot.*
> — Charlie Chaplin

Part I:
Get Ready for Take-Off

## Common Sense from a Child

Children can be wonderful teachers when it comes to dealing with any kind of airline upset.

An article in *USA Today*, for example, told of one young child who gave other passengers a lesson in how to deal with turbulence. The five-year-old boy, traveling with his mom, was dressed like a cowboy. When the plane hit a pocket of air during some bad weather, most of the adults gripped their armrests. Not this youngster, though. He grabbed his hat, tossed it into the air, and shouted YEEE HA!

I learned a great lesson from some children one day when my very early morning flight was canceled. While standing in line to be reticketed, I noticed how kids were reacting to the situation. They simply took out their Mutant Ninja Turtles toys, sat on the floor, and had fun playing. The adults, on the other hand, were moaning and groaning about the inconvenience.

What the children did was use the extra time to enjoy themselves.

You, too, can be creative in any airline adversity. Find something enjoyable to do instead of complaining. And be prepared, in advance, like the children. Bring something you can enjoy. Do not do work! Enjoy your crossword puzzle, write a postcard to your family and friends, or simply people-watch. The rest of the trip will be easier.

## Common Sense Rules #1, 2, & 3:

*Never yell at a ticket agent.*

**Never yell at a ticket agent.**

***Never yell at a ticket agent.***

When your flight is delayed or canceled, please don't yell at airport personnel. While circumstances may be difficult, this doesn't mean you must be out of control. Ranting, raving, or screaming when travel goes awry or bags go astray won't change the situation, but it can make matters worse. Remember, the ticketing agents and baggage handlers are the ones who have complete power over where you or your bags go.

Terry Paulson, a professional speaker and trainer, tells a story about a passenger he saw yelling at the curbside baggage handler. Despite his being barraged with anger, the handler remained perfectly calm. After the passenger left the scene, Paulson asked the man how he stayed unruffled in the face of such rage. The airline employee replied, "I just checked in his bags. He's going to Chicago. His bags are going to Japan."

Although some flight attendants probably don't want this known, they have confided in me that they know how to get even with extremely rude passengers.

One attendant said, when a particularly obnoxious passenger went to the restroom, she took the handkerchief from his coat pocket, put several lipstick imprints on it, and then returned it to his jacket. (He is probably still wondering where the marks came from . . . and so is his wife.)

Another attendant claims she got back at a very unpleasant customer by lacing his coffee with Ex Lax®.

Part I:
Get Ready for Take-Off

**Travel Secret: Be Nice to Airport Personnel**

# Chapter 1
## Dr. Travel Prescribes: Common Sense

On one of the flights taken by Brian Cassidy of Hyatt Corporation, a passenger entered First Class as the outside cabin door was closing and the stairway removed. He fell into the first seat — row 1 on the aisle — and demanded a drink. The flight attendant informed him that the plane was moving. Under FAA rules, no drinks could be served until after takeoff.

The passenger yelled at the flight attendant: "How come he has a drink and I don't?"

Again, the flight attendant reminded him drinks had been served prior to the plane leaving the gate and those drinks were being picked up as they spoke.

"Do you know who I am?" the passenger asked. "Do you know who I am?" he repeated.

The flight attendant continued to pick up the remaining drinks. "Do you know who I am? Do you know who I am?" the passenger continued to bellow.

Finally, the flight attendant picked up the microphone and announced: "Attention please! We have someone in First Class who doesn't know who he is. Can anyone come to the First Class cabin to identify him?"

For the remainder of the flight, nothing but silence came from the aisle seat in row one.

> *If you are patient in one moment of anger, you will escape a hundred days of sorrow.*
> — Chinese proverb

## Common Sense Rule #4:

Fixing a mechanical problem on the ground is better than fixing it when the plane is in the air.

## Common Sense Rule #5:

Being down here wishing you were up there is much better than being up there wishing you were down here.

## Common Sense Rule #6:

- If you are on a business trip, look like it.
- If you are on a pleasure trip, look like you are on a business trip.
- Always have business cards available.
- Print both sides of your business card to describe the products or services you offer. Or, mention some aspect of your business that may not be known from reading the front of your card. (Frequent travelers to a foreign country — especially Japan — print their business card in another language.)

## Common Sense Rule #7:

Never buy flight insurance. Not only is it expensive, but the chances of your dying in an airplane crash are slim. And how will your family know you bought flight insurance? Unless you mailed the policy to your home before your flight, you have the policy with you.

## Common Sense Rule #8:

If the deal seems too good to be true, it probably is.

- Beware of Internet giveaway notices and other travel deals.
- Do not pay any money without checking into company policies on refunds and cancellations.

- Get it in writing.
- Check with the Better Business Bureau. Refuse to do business with any firm that asks for unnecessary personal information.
- Never, never respond to pressure. Legitimate travel offers do not require instant responses.

## Common Sense Rule #9:

Designate a separate briefcase as your Office-on-the-Go. Or, make up a kit of personal items you need to take on any trip, so you won't have to repack each time you travel.

- Keep a list of trip-related items near your desk, so a week before you leave, you can refill your kit or briefcase.
- Include overnight express forms and fax cover sheets so you can send completed work back to your office.

*If you can't fight and you can't flee, flow.*
— Robert S. Eliot

## Common Sense Rule #10:

Put all receipts in one place. Take your office expense form with you and complete it as expenses are incurred. I use a separate folder for each specific meeting. Inside each folder is a zip-lock bag, courtesy of United Parcel Service (UPS). UPS offers these bags for overseas documents and each bag has glue on the back so it adheres to the file folder. Everything stays in one place.

## Common Sense Rule #11:

Hire a car and driver if your budget allows. You won't get lost and you can work or make calls, which may make your entire trip more productive.

Part I:
Get Ready for Take-Off

## Common Sense Rule #12:

Never tell your client you flew First Class, have a car and driver, or are staying in a suite. If you have to ask why, please return this book.

## Common Sense Rule #13:

### Shi<sup>f</sup>t Happens!®

- Always check on security briefings in troubled areas. The U.S. State Department is a comprehensive source, as are companies specializing in these types of briefings.
- Always check the weather forecast.
- Always call to confirm the flight is on time.
- Always have a Plan B.

## Travel Secret: Things Could Be Worse

Try changing your grimace into a grin by asking yourself how the situation could be worse. The next time you are upset about some airline-related adversity, remember things could always be worse. Take, for example, this it's-so-sad-it's-funny story from *Condé Nast Traveler* magazine:

Jeff Hoffman of Houston was trapped in the middle seat of a five-seat center row on a jam-packed flight. Tiring of his seatmate who hadn't showered, Hoffman turned to the passenger on the other side, whose baby promptly threw up all over his shirt. Hoffman went to the lavatory to wash off his shirt. On his way back, a woman fainted into his arms.

A passenger, thinking Hoffman was behaving indecently with a girlfriend, summoned a flight attendant. She arrived to find Hoffman and the woman on the ground, her head in his lap and his shirt soaked. Not understanding the situation, the attendant began reprimanding Hoffman in front of the crowd that had formed. 'I wanted to open the emergency door and jump out,' said Hoffman.

> *Most folks are about as happy as they make up their minds to be.*
> — Abraham Lincoln

Karyn Buxman from Hannibal, Missouri, gives us another example. Karen says, "I found myself in the Denver airport on an unscheduled layover. What was supposed to be a 35-minute wait became two hours, then another hour, then three more hours, then two more hours, then another hour, then another, and another. I was stuck in that airport for an extra ten hours. I was not a happy camper. So after fuming for a while I asked myself: How could this be worse? I decided, that for me, it would be worse to be stuck in the airport and be pregnant. How about nine months pregnant? And in active labor. I could be nine months pregnant, in active labor, stuck in this terminal with my water breaking in front of all these strangers! Absurd perhaps, but a vivid enough mental picture to force me to crack a smile and change my view of the situation."

## Travel Secret: Keep Things in Perspective

President Theodore Roosevelt and naturalist William Beebe had a ritual they would do each night on their after-dinner walks together. One of them would look up at the stars and declare: "That is the Spiral Galaxy of Andromeda, which is as large as our Milky Way. It is one of a hundred million galaxies and 750,000 light years away. It consists of one-hundred billion suns, each larger than our sun." Then there was silence. Finally, one of them would say, "Now I think we are small enough. Let's go to bed."

Keep things in perspective. Your delay or canceled flight may seem like the most important thing in the world to you. Yet, in the big picture, it is only a small occurrence in your life. You would be a fortunate person, indeed, if all your problems involved only a delay of a few hours . . . make the best of it.

Part I:
Get Ready for Take-Off

*He who would travel happily must travel light.*
— Antoine de Saint-Exupéry

## Chapter 2
# A Sense of Humor

"Next to common sense," says author Mark McCormack in his book, *What They Don't Teach You at Harvard Business School*, "the most important thing in business is a sense of humor." The business of air travel is no different.

Humor gives perspective and a way of getting the upper-hand on any unexpected or uncontrollable situation. Humor is an invaluable tool in dealing with airline adversities.

"Angels can fly because they take themselves lightly," G. K. Chesterton said. You, too, can soar above the crowds of disgruntled passengers if you learn to lighten up about the not-so-funny world of airline travel.

### Travel Secret: Pack Perky Pick-Me-Ups

When you were young, you probably never went far without your old blankie, teddy, or favorite toy. You still can take them. If you think this is a childish idea, read on.

Part I:
Get Ready for Take-Off

Britain's Prince Charles never journeys without his worn-out teddy bear. And a U.S. newspaper recently reported that hotels around the country reported seeing stuffed animals and well-worn baby blankets in rooms occupied only by traveling business people.

So remember to pack a picture of your pet, a warm fuzzy, or a wind-up toy to add a sense of security and fun to your trip.

> *It's all right to have a good time. That's one of the most important messages of enlightenment.*
> — Thaddeus Golas,
> *The Lazy Man's Guide to Enlightenment*

## Travel Secret: Goofs Become Giggles

We all make silly mistakes. Instead of trying to hide your faux pas, learn to celebrate them. In Paris once, author Allen Klein mistakenly entered a restaurant by the back door and barged in on a private party of twenty-five businessmen having dinner. he was embarrassed by his blunder, but managed to recover quickly. As he paraded through the room, he bowed politely and wished them all a hearty "Bon Appétit!"

In a hotel in China, he stood for ten minutes impatiently pressing the button of the elevator until someone informed him it was the switch for the lights down the hall.

Late one evening, while traveling in Europe, Allen headed for the local supermarket. When he got to the parking lot, he saw an entire family make a mad dash out of their car and run toward the store. Thinking it must be near closing time and not wanting to be shut out, he jogged in right behind them. When they entered the store, they all ran into the bathroom!

## Chapter 2
## Dr. Travel Prescribes: A Sense of Humor

*Humor is the traveler's first line of defense. Travel without humor is like sex without love. You can do it, but what's the point really?*

— Mary Morris

## Travel Secret: Wear Something Unusual

Every holiday, Pat Harrington, a flight attendant Allen Klein met while traveling, wears something funny relating to that specific time of year, such as an amusing Christmas pin, a humorous Easter button, or a leprechaun face. Pat finds this helps establish a light-hearted bond with her passengers.

"Dressing-up" can help add some light-heartedness to your travel day, too. Here, for example, is a letter humor educator Allen Klein received from one of his workshop attendees:

Dear Mr. Klein:

I want to tell you about an incident that happened to me after being in one of your workshops. I had to take a trip I did not want to take. I was grumpy about it and became more upset as the days got closer to my leaving.

So I decided I would turn my negativity around. I went to my local thrift shop and got the baggiest brightest pair of pants I could find, some red suspenders, and a big polka-dotted shirt. Then I bought an inexpensive multicolored wig. Your red clown nose from the workshop topped off my costume.

The day of the trip I was regretting turned into one of the best days of my life. When I got to the airport in my clown outfit, some kids came over and asked for my autograph. One man was convinced he had seen me recently in the

Part I:
Get Ready for Take-Off

Ringling Brothers circus. Best of all, when they announced the boarding of my flight, they said, "We are going to begin preboarding only. Those needing a little extra time — families with children and clowns — may go first."

Judy Streitmatter<br>South Bend, Indiana

If such an outward display of frivolity is not right for you, get an inner chuckle by wearing something no one else can see — like some wildly outrageous underwear.

I always wear a pin. I carry extras for those who seem interested in the content or who provide extra service to me or a fellow passenger on a trip. I have two different pins: one reads **ATTITUDE** and the other reads **Shift Happens!**® Both pins mean I have an attention-getting device. By wearing the pin on my right lapel that reads ATTITUDE, I explain I have the right ATTITUDE . . . and everyone wants it. The pin on my left lapel that reads **Shift Happens!**® makes people smile. You all know its real meaning, but this pin conveys the message that change does happen, no matter how we try to control our lives. Travel with the right attitude and the knowledge that travel is not a perfect science. Just don't volunteer as the guinea pig.

*We all thank you for flying the friendly skies. All of us hope you will choose us again. Including my children's orthodontist.*

— United Flight attendant

## Travel Secret: Pretend You're on "Totally Hidden Videos"

Make believe a video camera is filming your every action. How do you look screaming at the counter clerk who can't seem to find your reservations?

After you see this picture, maybe you'll want to change the channel to a more pleasant one.

## Travel Secret: Take a Lesson from Flight Attendants

If you think you have problems with airline travel, think of airline personnel. You are dealing with one problem. Sometimes they deal with hundreds of frustrated and angry passengers.

Take a lesson from them. During adverse conditions, flight attendants often manage to keep their sense of humor and use it to calm passengers, ease tension, and make everyone's trip more pleasant. For example, at the end of one long and crowded flight, the flight attendant botched up the prelanding announcement. She misread words, gave the wrong time, and announced the wrong city we were about to land in. The attendant saved the day with some humor when she ended her announcement with "This message has been prerecorded."

> *If you liked today's flight, it was United 240. If you didn't, it was Delta 89.*
> — United Flight attendant

Here are some other examples of how flight attendants have used humor during trying times.

Maalox moment: A long delay before take-off.

Sense of humor solution: "Ladies and gentlemen. We are currently number 524 for take-off. We should be off the ground in about 6 hours, 43 minutes, and 32 seconds."

Maalox moment: An extremely short layover.

Sense of humor solution: "Welcome to Albuquerque. If you are continuing on this flight to El Paso and you wish to leave the plane, please take your boarding pass with you. You'll need it to reboard. The local time is 1:40 P.M. We depart at 1:41 P.M. You have one minute."

Maalox moment: The flight was canceled after all the passengers were seated because of a mechanical problem. The passengers must get off the inoperable plane and reboard exactly the same type of plane at the next gate.

Sense of humor solution: "Ladies and gentlemen, welcome to Déja Vu Airlines."

Maalox moment: The passengers were not paying attention to the safety instructions.

Sense of humor solution #1: "The captain has placed a $20 bill in one of your safety instruction booklets, so please take it out and look at it."

Sense of humor solution #2: "There are fifty ways to leave your lover, but only four ways to leave this aircraft. Please look for those exits."

## You Are Noble and Should Be Rewarded.

While travelling on an American flight from Chicago to San Antonio, I saw a young couple board the plane only to find they were not sitting together. Seeing how distraught they were, I offered to give up my seat. They were elated!

During the meal service the flight attendant from First Class came to my seat to thank me for "my noble deed."

She offered to buy me a drink because coach charges for their drinks. I declined, stating I "did not drink." She flashed a wonderful smile, thanked me again, and left.

About ten minutes after coach meals were cleared, the flight

# Chapter 2
## Dr. Travel Prescribes: A Sense of Humor

attendant presented herself again. This time she had two hot Mrs. Fields® Cookies. She put down my tray table, smiled, and said, "You eat don't you?"

### Northwest Orients Its Passengers

"Not long ago, my wife Mary was on a Northwest flight with a cabin crew who sounded like they were auditioning for a local comedy club," says Jon Hanson/Direct Data. Mary said that the jokes were funny, and they were carefully focused for experienced travellers. The passengers were amused and entertained throughout the flight, but the best line came after the aircraft landed and was taxiing to the gate.

The lead steward got on the PA system and began the oft repeated speech about destinations, gate locations, and the service people waiting to help you. Then, as the plane approached the gate and passengers were becoming restless to stand earlier than allowed, the steward uttered these classic lines. He said. "Northwest has invested a lot of money to be sure your flight has been safe and comfortable. We are also looking for ways to save money and this aircraft is participating in a new experiment. To reduce costs, we are asking for volunteers to help clean up the cabin after we stop. All those wishing to volunteer for cabin clean-up, please stand up before we come to a full stop." Not a single passenger left his or her seat before the seat belt sign was turned off.

As far as I know, flight attendants do not take stand-up comedy classes. Yet, over and over again, I have witnessed their skilled use of humor to lighten-up weighty circumstances.

Take a lesson from these masters of airline mirth and you too can be flying the happy skies.

> *Laughter and tears are both responses to frustration and exhaustion. I myself prefer to laugh, since there is less cleaning up to do afterward.*
> — Kurt Vonnegut, Jr.

Part I:
Get Ready for Take-Off

## The Groaners of Today Are the Grins of Tomorrow

It has been said that humor is tragedy plus time. What seems like an awful situation at the moment often seems laughable later.

Betsy Morscher, an author and international spa consultant, describes her not-so-funny-now-funny-later experience: "I had just arrived in Boston after making two plane connections and was on the third lap of a trip to speak in Connecticut." Dressed in her finest clothing, complete with matching picture hat, she proceeded to put her bag in an overhead compartment.

"As I reached up," she says, "my purse flew open and the contents fell on a man seated below. When I bent down to pick up my belongings, my umbrella handle hooked the man across the aisle causing him to drop his newspaper. In the process of retrieving it, he inadvertently knocked his seat mate's briefcase and all its contents on the floor."

Morscher concludes about this Rube Goldberg-like scene, "a couple sitting across the aisle asked me if I fly this route often because they do, and they had never laughed so hard."

In *You Can't Afford the Luxury of a Negative Thought*, author John-Roger writes about finding humor at the airport. "Once I was traveling to give a lecture. The plane was late, and everyone else's luggage came off before ours. Somewhere across town, there were several hundred people in a rented hall waiting for me to give a talk — perhaps on the importance of being on time — and it was getting later and later. Finally our luggage started to arrive. (We were carrying our own sound equipment, so it wouldn't have done much good to go on ahead.) One suitcase had sprung open, and clothes were spread all over the conveyer belt. Another piece of luggage was obviously damaged. The people traveling with me were getting more and more upset.

Finally I said, 'Relax, this is funny. In a few weeks we'll be

## Chapter 2
### Dr. Travel Prescribes: A Sense of Humor

telling stories about tonight and laughing about it. If it'll be funny then, it's funny now.' And we started looking at the situation as if it were a Woody Allen movie. When some of the luggage didn't arrive, we smiled. When the car rental company didn't have our reservation (or cars), we laughed. When we heard there was a taxi strike, we howled."

> *Laughter is the shortest distance between two people.*
> — Victor Borge

To prove that the tough travel tales of today can become the laughs of tomorrow, one company in New Jersey (the Executive Communications Group) gives out an annual travel award for the worst travel horror story.

Richard Cole of Hartford, Connecticut won one year. He reported that his luggage was lost on a flight. Nothing new or funny about that except that he was the only passenger on board.

*Executive Travel* magazine asked for similar worst flying experiences from their readers. The winning entry stated: "Officials, after discovering a domestic West African flight had been grossly overbooked, asked all passengers with boarding cards to run twice around the plane. The fastest ones got the seats." You may not be able to top these winners, but by laughing at your own travel horror stories, you'll win the less-stress game every time.

> *If you listen carefully to children you will have plenty about which to laugh.*
> — Steve Allen

Part I:
Get Ready for Take-Off

## Go Ahead, Make Your Day

A colleague of mine once participated in a closed-circuit teleconference with Norman Cousins, the noted author/celebrity who healed himself of a life-threatening illness with humor. Cousins said hospitals are often stress producing environments and it is part of the patient's responsibility to cheer things up.

Cousins told a story about the time a nurse came into his room to get a urine sample. She handed him a jar and said she would be right back. He poured some apple juice in it and waited. When the nurse returned, Cousins held the specimen up to the light and exclaimed, "This looks a bit cloudy. I think it needs recycling." Then he gulped it down.

Cousins knew that helping to amuse the staff also helped to amuse him.

Sometimes airports and airplanes seem like hospitals. They are not always the most cheery of places, lots of people are scurrying around and often, like a hospital, it's a hurry-up-and-wait world.

Perhaps, like Cousins' approach, you might try lightening up someone else's day. It may actually make your day brighter, too.

## Letter from the United Pilot

On a recent trip to Hawaii, I was upgraded to First Class using my upgrade certificates which I earned as a frequent flyer. About two hours into the flight, the flight attendant presented each person in the cabin with an envelope with our name on the envelope. Inside we found a letter addressed to each passenger, by name.

This was a letter, from the captain of this aircraft thanking us for flying with United. Most important, it was a true expression of a pilot-owner to his customers. The pilot mentioned he appreciated our business. For almost the next hour, the twelve people in First Class spoke about the gesture and the deterioration of service and quality of other airlines. Not one person had anything derogatory to say about United. Funny how a little customer service goes a long way.

Chapter 2
Dr. Travel Prescribes: A Sense of Humor

## Kids Say the Darndest Things

If you are looking for a laugh during stressful travel moments, seek out some children. The funniest lines often come from the mouths of babes.

Comedian Michael Pritchard, for example, once saw a child waiting to greet his mother who was emerging from the jetway. With his father standing next to him, the child bellowed, "Hi Mom! While you were gone nobody slept with Dad!"

One time, when I was standing in line to be reticketed, I could not help but overhear the conversation of two children. One of them turned to the other and in a very loud voice shouted, "Aren't you pissed at the airlines?" Not only did they give the adults around them a good belly laugh, but they expressed exactly what most of us were feeling.

You may not be able to shout out how you feel in front of hundreds of people, but you can choose a technique children often use when they don't like their situation. You can, like a child, play in your mind. For example, the next time you have an airline upset, pretend you are in some Broadway musical and silently sing some "mind-songs" to cheer yourself. Here are some suggestions:

- "Put on a Happy Face" (from *Bye Bye Birdie*)
- "The Sun Will Come Out Tomorrow" (from *Annie*)
- "I Want to Be Happy" (from *No, No, Nanette*)
- "Whistle a Happy Tune" (from *The King and I*)
- "Happy Talk" (from *South Pacific*)

or these popular songs

- "On Top of the World"
- "Walking on Sunshine"
- "Tell Him You Love Him"
- "Sound of Music"

Part I:
Get Ready for Take-Off

## Travel Secret: Increase Your Smileage

If you can't find any laughter in a situation, remember to at least smile. When you smile, the world smiles back.

"Smiles and frowns," says Dr. Jerry Teplitz, a stress specialist, "affect people whether we are aware of it or not. If you are in an airport where nobody wants to be, and planes are running really late, literally the energy of everyone around you is affecting you."

Smiling is important, whether or not you have anything to smile about. Research has shown that your body doesn't know the difference between a real smile and a fake one. So even if you don't feel like smiling, do it anyway. It triggers a time when you were smiling for real (like when the plane actually left on time).

Allen Klein suggests this: Put a pen or pencil in your mouth (no, not the point or the eraser, the flat side, please) and push it as far back as you can. Now take the pen or pencil out of your mouth while still holding your face in the position you just created. There, you have faked your face into forming a smile. Keep your face in that smile position and your body will soon get the hint.

## Chapter 2
### Dr. Travel Prescribes: A Sense of Humor

## Travel Secret: Jest for the Fun of It

Have yourself paged on the white courtesy phone.

Give up your seat and stay in the airport on purpose.

Sometimes I think passengers forget their brains when they travel. Somehow the logical solutions to nonlogical questions escape them. These are real questions:

Why are my bags always the last to come off the plane?

What do the three-letter codes mean on my baggage tag?

Why are they there? Can't they spell the name of the city?

Which is the best luggage to buy? And in what color?

*A smiling face will get you a great deal more than a stomping foot.*
— V. Neil Wyrick

Part I:
Get Ready for Take-Off

*A hundred years ago, it could take you the better part of a year to get from New York to California, whereas today, because of equipment problems at O'Hare, you can't get there at all.*

— Dave Barry

# Chapter 3
# A Sense of Adventure

Picture this: You have a 6:33 a.m. flight from the West Coast to the East Coast with a change of planes in Chicago. Your ride to the airport is scheduled to pick you up at 5:05 a.m. (Yes this is early, but at least you won't have to worry about getting to the airport on time and you'll have a chance to get some coffee.)

You are up at 4:30 a.m., showered, dressed, and ready to go before five. At 5:17 a.m. , no shuttle is in sight, so you telephone the van service. After being put on hold for almost ten minutes (don't you hate the calming music they play at times like this?), you are told the bad news — the computer does not have your reservation. The good news, though, is a van in the area can pick you up in about ten minutes.

Eighteen and a half minutes later, no ride is in sight. Frantically, you call again. You are assured the shuttle will be there "any minute."

At 5:46 a.m., your ride finally arrives. You feel a bit more relaxed knowing the ride to the airport is fairly short, but with traffic and another passenger to pick up, you arrive only seven minutes before your flight is scheduled to leave.

So much for coffee. You know the only hope of catching your flight is to make a mad dash to the gate along with the two overstuffed pieces of luggage you planned to check.

You arrive just as they are closing the door to the jet way. You

Part I:
Get Ready for Take-Off

make the plane. You manage to find a place in the overhead bins for at least one piece of luggage (today must be your lucky day!) and you sink down in your seat — exhausted, but relieved. As soon as the plane is airborne, you know you will get your coffee.

When the captain announces a slight mechanical problem has occurred, you realize that cup of coffee may take a little longer than you thought. "It will take only a few minutes to fix and we'll be on our way," the captain assures you.

Thirty minutes later, this minor mechanical problem has turned into a major one. You begin to think this may not be your lucky day after all and comfort yourself by thinking, *Wasn't I going to give up coffee anyway?*

You only have a thirty-five minute connection in Chicago. If the plane doesn't leave this instant, you will miss your next flight. It doesn't and you do.

To make matters worse, your luggage never made it on to the second flight ("But we'll definitely deliver it to you between 2 A.M. and 5 A.M.," the airline promises). The cab driver gets hopelessly lost ("I thought you said The Postmark, not The Mark Post") and the hotel gave your room to someone else ("But we can put you up in a hotel a few miles away and transfer you in the morning").

You finally doze off at 2:07 A.M. thinking, *Well, maybe this is my lucky day after all. It's only 11:07 P.M. on the West Coast!*

# Chapter 3
## Dr. Travel Prescribes: A Sense of Adventure

*Inconvenience is an adventure misunderstood.*
— Zen saying

## Travel Secret: Expect the Unexpected

"Travelers in 1492," notes V. Neil Wyrick, from Miami, Florida, "did not expect exquisite cuisine or well-kept schedules. They were delighted to arrive alive. When Christopher Columbus set sail from the port of Palos, he knew to expect the unexpected. There were those who warned him that if he sailed too far west he would fall off the world and be swallowed up by monsters at sea. His pitifully small ships could have been smashed by huge storms or pillaged by pirates. And while things are much improved for today's traveler, it's best to expect the unexpected."

Matt Weinstein, cofounder of Play Fair, tells of the unexpected adventure he encountered at Chicago's O'Hare airport. Weinstein was standing in line to buy a ticket to Dallas. The woman in front of him was also buying a ticket to Dallas, but she was having some kind of problem. The reservationist asked the woman to step aside until they took care of the other passengers. When Weinstein got to his gate, the same woman approached him.

"Did you get your ticket handled?" Weinstein asked. "No," the woman replied, "I didn't. I got mugged last night. They took everything — my driver's license and credit cards. So I called my uncle who lives in Dallas and he wired me a prepaid ticket, but something went wrong with the airline computer." The woman continued, "The airline shows my reservation, but they don't show the ticket is prepaid. This is the last flight out tonight. I don't have money for a hotel and I'm going to have to spend the whole night here at the airport."

"So," Weinstein said, "I thought to myself, OK, one of two possible things is going on here. The first possibility is this is a poor stranded woman and I don't want to leave her here at the airport overnight. And the second is she's a con artist."

Part I:
Get Ready for Take-Off

After talking to the woman a while, Weinstein decided she was, indeed, telling the truth and bought her a ticket to Dallas. In return, she promised to stop by his hotel at 9 A.M. the next morning to repay him.

The next morning came and went with no word from the woman. The rest of the day went by. Still no word. So Weinstein called the business number she'd given him. After numerous rings, someone finally answered, but no one had ever heard of the woman at this company. "I realized," Weinstein said. "I had just been ripped off by a professional scam artist with a very elaborate story." Weinstein continued, "I also realized I had just seen one of the greatest theatrical performances of all times. Of course, I usually don't pay $340 a ticket. Then again, I usually don't get to sit that close either!"

## Oh Goodie ... Another Adventure!

When I was young, my neighbor took me to the airport to see passengers board a propeller plane and then fly off into the clouds. The experience of seeing an aircraft take off was so thrilling, no one thought of leaving the observation deck before the flight was airborne. In those days, flying was exciting for those on the plane, as well as for those watching from below. Today, I compare the same level of mystery to the introduction of a new car model. Years ago, this was a major event. Today, not unlike walking on the moon, we hardly take notice.

*Life is always subject to negotiation.*
— Richard Weinstein,
Carnival Cruise Lines

# Chapter 3
## Dr. Travel Prescribes: A Sense of Adventure

Millions of Americans currently travel by air each year. The observers of yesteryear have become planeloads of unhappy passengers. Air travel has become so routine, most of its excitement is gone.

But my conviction is this: Some of the former sense of excitement can still be found, if you can reformat the adversities of air travel and see them as adventures. I have found that adequate preparation is always a great stress reliever. When I fly, I always read the airline magazine. You know the ones with a welcome from the president or chairman of the airline addressing some issue that may or may not be relevant to you. In each magazine, I find several sources of information necessary reading.

The first is the section containing the music and movie listings. As soon as I board the plane, in the coach section, the flight attendants announce the news they will happily rent you headphones for slightly less than a first-run movie theater ticket. How can you make an informed decision if you are not informed? Read the section describing the movies, as well as the music, books on tape, healing powers, yoga, Zen, and Tai Chi lessons you can use to reduce stress while flying.

The second section is the map of the airport gates. This information is quite useful if you want to get from the gate at which you land to the one you need to connect for the ongoing flight. If you are flying to a destination without connections, congratulations! You probably read the section on a direct versus a nonstop flight.

The third section is the short article detailing an itinerary for a specific city. Naturally you are not going to this city, but it still makes fascinating reading. United Airlines calls this minitour guide "Three Perfect Days." "Three Perfect Days," as United says in its ads, "eliminates the guesswork and offers an elegant, authoritative itinerary designed by a sophisticated and savvy local. But it's knowing about all those places only the locals know about that makes the Three Perfect Days experience so special." Cities such as Bangkok, Beijing, Berlin, Budapest, Kyoto, Lima, Santiago, and

Part I:
Get Ready for Take-Off

Shanghai are just a few of the far away world-class cities that United's hometown writers have examined. Now let me ask you, "When was the last time you found yourself in New Delhi with only three days to be a tourist?" And, more important, why did you go without knowing what to do, where to eat, or what not to say prior to leaving? Personally, I love the concept of the article, but this is information that is unavailable at the time I need it.

United will sell you a copy of the article (check or money order only) for $3.50 (U.S.) per destination or for $10 (U.S.), they will rush it to you, 2nd day priority mail. Wouldn't you think they would offer it free on the Internet, or fax on demand, or have a reference copy of all the articles on the airplane? Here, for once, is a service the airline could offer its passengers. How often do you think the average person plans a trip to Sydney for a few days and does not have time to get any information about the destination? Atlanta, Baltimore, Boston, Charleston, Chicago, Los Angeles, and Miami all get written up in the same manner and for the same cost.

> *Adventures challenge us and stretch us, they teach us and open us up — and, if we are lucky, they make us wiser and fuller, more attentive, and more accepting, human beings.*
> — Donald W. George, travel editor,
> San Francisco *Examiner*

Here is an excellent "incentive" item for Mileage Plus or AAdvantage Miles to offer its customers: enable them to call a special number or access fax on demand by putting in their Frequent Flyer Number for points to be deducted. Instant information, as needed, by those who need it. And at the end of the year, a copy of the twelve cities can be sent out to frequent flyers who travel more than 50,000 miles per year (or other criteria).

In *The Healing Power of Humor*, author Allen Klein writes about a woman who was having one personal problem after another. Just as she was near her wit's end, the water heater in her house blew up.

# Chapter 3
## Dr. Travel Prescribes: A Sense of Adventure

No major damage occurred, but there was plenty to clean up. As she began to tackle the task, her young son came running into the room and loudly exclaimed, "Oh, good, we're having another adventure!"

*Webster's Dictionary* defines an adventure as "an unusual and stirring experience." Air travel frequently fits this definition. It gives you unusual experiences that stir your emotions (like being stranded at an out-of-the-way airport) and typical of an adventure, you are never quite certain what will happen next. To top things off, airlines make you the star of this drama. You would probably pay good money to see this kind of excitement at the movies! The airlines, however, often throw in a free real-life adventure included in the cost of your ticket. And to add even more spice to your adventure, airlines also add frequent flyer points so you can fly more often on the very same airline that served terrible food, lost your baggage, and kept you in Wichita overnight when you wanted to be in St. Louis.

Although your itinerary says what time you are supposed to arrive, you really never know for certain what time you will arrive. For example, you may get to your destination five hours after the scheduled time, you may wind up in a completely different city than you expected, or you may never get off the ground.

## Airline Red Carpet Treatment

Several of the advantages of flying First Class are you get the best service, the best food, more comfortable seats, and you can meet some very interesting passengers. I have flown with Robert Redford, Buddy Hackett, Suzanne Somers, Brian Tracy, Harry Blackstone Jr., O. J. Simpson, F. Lee Bailey, Bryant Gumble, and Jay Leno, among others. But you needn't pay for the most expensive ticket to have an adventure.

Part I:
Get Ready for Take-Off

While waiting in the Red Carpet Club for a flight at the Los Angeles airport, I noticed I was alone. The entire room was empty. The silence was suddenly broken by the sound of eight children running into the room — yelling, screaming, and changing the TV channels. As I began to reprimand them, the most soothing voice and the most lovely face came into view. "Excuse the youngens," the woman said. Dolly Parton stood before me. Without a doubt, Dolly is one of the most spectacularly beautiful woman I have ever seen in person. Wearing a checked red and white shirt tied above her tiny waist and below her large . . . well, you know. Looking and listening at the same time was difficult. Her smile lights a room, her voice is more soothing than ocean waves against the sand, and her figure is the stuff of which dreams are made. How could you not excuse anything an angel requests?

Dolly sat down and offered to buy me drink. She offered to leave the room and take the "youngens" with her. Naturally I could not let her sit in the general seating area of the airport terminal. It was, as they say, not the gentlemanly thing to do. So I endured. For nearly two hours, I experienced pleasant company and visual stimulation. I saw Dolly off to her plane. Then I realized my flight had long since departed.

> *There is no such thing as a problem without a gift for you in its hands. You seek problems because you need their gifts.*
> — Richard Bach

I returned to the Red Carpet Club staff who recognized me as the "saint" who kept all the children out of the general seating area. They found a seat for me on the next flight and, to make it up to me, they provided a First Class seat instead of the coach seat I'd purchased. The moral here? Always keep out the red carpet.

You can see your trials and tribulations of travel as aggravation or, as in the movies or through a child's eyes, you can see them as an adventure. The choice is yours. Do your homework and let the adventure begin.

> *Be Prepared.*
> — Boy Scout Motto

## The Physcial Preparation

Now that you've promised yourself never to leave home without your three senses, you need to make many other decisions about your trip. Not only must you decide about such major things as when to book your ticket, which carrier to use, and what to pack, you must also resolve less vital — but still important — comfort-influencing decisions. Should you board early to snatch overhead bin space or board late to avoid sitting any longer than necessary in a cabin filled with stale air? Should you get an aisle seat where you can bop up and down or choose a window seat where you must be double-jointed to climb over your seat mate(s)? The remainder of this section focuses on your physical preparations.

Part I:
Get Ready for Take-Off

*Please Go Away!*
— A sign at a travel agency

*See the World Before You Leave It.*
— Another sign at a travel agency

## Chapter 4
# Choosing a Travel Agent

I know one business person who calls the airlines to book all his flights. He phones as many as five airlines to get their different schedules and to compare prices. This is difficult, time-consuming, and unnecessary. A good travel agent can do all your planning and ticketing for you . . . and more.

The good news is a travel agent has nearly all the airline schedules and costs. The other good news is an agent does not charge any more than if you booked your ticket directly with the airline (travel agents get their commissions from the airline, hotel, or car rental company).

Although there's no really bad news about using a travel agent, perhaps one drawback does exist: most travel agents are not open twenty-four hours a day. If you must travel on short notice and your travel agency is closed, you have two options. You can either call the airline directly or use one of the computer online services to book your flight (perhaps the latter is the better choice because you can compare costs and schedules without making numerous calls). With this in mind, many long-distance carriers include a 24-hour travel service as part of their premium services to entice members to use their phone cards.

Other than this, there's no reason to avoid using a travel agent.

Part I:
Get Ready for Take-Off

> *Do you recall as a child being told by your mother that the policeman is your friend? This is, admittedly, a difficult sentiment to cling to as the nice officer writes you a $100 ticket for speeding in a school zone. What your mother could have said (yeah, we will go farther: should have said) is that your best friend, if you only knew it, is your friendly neighborhood travel agent.*
> — Terry and Rocky Denton

## Travel Secret: Why You Need a Travel Agent

- Travel agents know more than you know about travel.

- Travel agents know your flying profile (your seat preference, special meals, frequent flyer number, and so forth), so you needn't repeat it each time you book a flight (as you would if you did your own bookings).

- Travel agents save you time. Let the agents do the walking. Because of their computer access, they know which airlines have the most convenient flights and connections.

- Travel agents give you more choices. When you call one carrier you only get that airline's itinerary and pricing. Agents have access to nearly all airlines. (I say nearly all because some smaller, low-fare, or charter airlines may not be on the agents' computer systems).

- Travel agents get preferential treatment — and you don't. Because of the volume of business travel agents do with the airlines, agents sometimes can clear a seat for you that may be unavailable if you call the airline directly.

- Travel agents are problem solvers. Good agents know the ticketing rules, restrictions, and how, if necessary, to get around them.

- Travel agents provide one-stop shopping. In addition to booking your airline tickets, agents can also obtain your car, hotel, train, and cruise ship reservations.

- Travel agents don't charge a penny extra for their services.

# Chapter 4
## Dr. Travel Prescribes: Choosing a Travel Agent

*The client/agent relationship is like any other relationship. It's like having a doctor or a dentist. You want someone who is your friend.*

— Marjorie Yasueda,
senior travel counselor

## Travel Secret: How to Find a Good Agent

Finding a good travel agent may take some searching. After all, he or she must be, among other things, a computer whiz, a world traveler, and a telephone maven. The effort you spend in looking for a good agent, however, will be well worth your time in the long run.

The best way to locate an agent is to ask your friends and co-workers which travel agent they use and what they like or dislike about this agent. Then interview these agents yourself. Ask the agents these questions:

- **How much experience do you have?**

This is a key question because the more travel-related experience agents have, the better they can serve you. Also, the answer to this question will give you additional insights into their special expertise (like having been a tour guide in China for ten years).

- **Do you travel a lot?**

Don't expect agents to have been everywhere. When you want a recommendation, though, agents who travel (as opposed to just travel agents) probably can give you better advice than those who work only from guidebooks.

- **Do you work in an office with other agents?**

You want a travel agent who works with other agents for two reasons: First, if your primary agent is busy or away from the office (agents travel often), someone else can help you immediately. Second, if your agent doesn't know the answer or isn't familiar with the area you plan to visit, another agent may know the area.

Part I:
Get Ready for Take-Off

## Travel Secret: Once You Find an Agent

- Stick with an agent, once you find one you like. Agents are apt to spend more time with repeat clients.

- If you are working with a large agency, get someone assigned to you so you get to know your agent and he or she gets to know your travel habits and idiosyncrasies.

- If your agent isn't getting you boarding passes in advance, find another agent.

- If you feel your agent isn't giving you enough time or effort, look elsewhere.

- Trust your gut. If you feel good about the relationship, continue it. If you don't, don't.

## Travel Secret: Become Your Own Agent

- Several travel agencies have offered independent travel agent status to the public. They provide you with an identification card, travel agent discounts for hotels and cruises, and, sometimes, even for airlines.

- Internet sales directly to the end user (you) are now being discounted. The airlines continue to reduce the commission they pay for domestic airline tickets. To buffer the reaction of travel agents, the airlines offer reduced fares over the Internet without commission. In some cases, these are cheaper than what is available through the travel agent network.

- Frequent flyer miles, cash discounts, direct booking, the Internet, reduced commissions, and more flights to more cities more frequently are only a few of the changes that have taken the travel industry into the twenty-first century. Change is now a major part of the methods used by marketing, sales, and distribution channels. Remember . . . **Shift Happens!**®

*Whenever possible, avoid airlines which have anyone's name in their titles, like Air Fred or Bob's International Airline.*

— Miss Piggy

## Chapter 5
# Choosing a Flight

United Airlines asks us to "Fly the friendly skies." American Airlines tells us they are "Something special in the air." And Delta Airlines says "We love to fly and it shows."

With such enticing advertising copy, how do you know which carrier to choose? To answer this question, you need to consider a number of factors and then decide which carrier is best for you.

Some of the things to consider when you choose a flight:

- price of ticket
- departure/arrival times
- nonstop/multistop versus change of plane
- aircraft type (older planes need more maintenance)
- frequent-flyer mileage rewards
- airline hub closest to your home
- best safety record
- current labor disputes or contract negotiations
- best on-time record

Part I:
Get Ready for Take-Off

This chapter, as well as some that follow, explores what you should know before you go. For instance, ask about a flight's on-time performance before booking it. Every airline is rated from 1 to 10: A number 1 means the airline arrives on schedule 10 percent of the time; a number 10 means the airline has an on-time record 100 percent of the time.

> *Departure time — Archaic phrase dating back to passenger-railroad days indicating a moment in time approximately three hours before takeoff.*
> — Michael Kilian

## ✈Travel Tip: Know Some Airline Lingo

Things are not always as they seem. What the airline ticket says may not show what it really means.

*Code sharing,* for example, is a way the airlines are using their alliances — their other airline partners — to book you on routes they do not fly.

You step off a jumbo jet and on to a turboprop flight, all the while thinking you were flying a major carrier for your entire route. Instead, the airlines have switched you to one of their partner's smaller commuter planes.

Other airline lingo is also confusing. You are booked, for example,

Chapter 5
Choosing a Flight

on a direct flight, so you board in one city and get off at your destination without stopping. Right? Wrong! A direct flight means you will be making one or more stops, but without changing planes. If you don't want to change planes, make sure you book a nonstop flight.

- A *nonstop flight* does not stop.
- A *direct flight* stops and then continues to your destination.
- A *connecting flight* requires you to change planes.
- A *through flight* involves both a change of aircraft and airline.
- A *delayed flight* means bring a good book to read or write one.
- A *missed flight* means the plane left without you.
- An *airline snack* means you better not be hungry.
- An *airline snack you pack yourself* means you better bring enough to share.
- A *coach meal* means you better eat before you fly.
- A *kid's meal* means it will be better than a coach meal — unless you ordered a special meal, which may mean a kid's meal. Try the hamburger or pizza — they are always good. After all, a kid will be upset if the food is bad and he or she will then upset others on the flight. Adults just eat the bad food and sulk.
- A *First Class meal* means you should not eat before the flight, unless it is a short flight where they serve you the same snack as coach, but you get linen instead of paper napkins. If a movie is being shown, you are assured of a full meal. If two movies are being shown, you will be unable to eat all the food presented throughout the flight.

> *Best airline? Any that gets me there on time, in one piece, and without indigestion.*
> — Pamela Fiori

Part I:
Get Ready for Take-Off

## ✈Travel Tip: Don't Set It Up for Failure

I once asked an attorney — who travels cross-country on a regular basis — his best tip for airline passengers. His answer? "Try not to set it up for failure."

For example, instead of going from Sacramento, California, to Washington, D.C., with a mandatory stopover in Chicago, this attorney drove one-and-one-half hours to San Francisco and got on a nonstop flight. This may be difficult to do sometimes with the spoke-and-hub system, but avoid changing planes whenever possible. Every change of plane means another chance for a delay or a canceled connection or lost luggage.

## ✈Travel Tip: Take the First — Avoid the Last

- Book the first flight of the day. When flights are delayed, they affect other connections. The earlier you leave, the more options you have.

- Avoid taking the last flight of the day if you must be at your destination the next morning. If your flight is canceled, you're stuck overnight.

- Reread *The Accidental Tourist*, by Anne Tyler, or rent the video.

## ✈Travel Tip: Nonstop Flights . . . the Best?

When you consider which flight to take, remember the more times you land and takeoff or change planes, the more you increase your chance for delays. If you must connect:

- Try to connect at a Sun Belt hub in the winter to avoid bad weather.

- Look for flights with stopovers at small airports. Reduced traffic also reduces delays.

- Allow at least one hour for connections.

## Chapter 5
### Dr. Travel Prescribes: Choosing a Flight

Although nonstops are generally the best way to avoid delays, times may occur when you want a connecting flight. For example, Joyce Cooper, a speaker/trainer from the state of Washington, tries to route her flights through Minneapolis. Her daughter and son-in-law live there and, when Joyce is passing through, they frequently meet her at the airport.

> *The Concorde is great. Traveling at twice the speed of sound is fun except you can't hear the movie till two hours after you land.*
> — Howie Mandel

> *There ain't no movies on Concorde, Howie, baby.*
> — Bart Smyth, world traveler

Because domestic flights allow up to four hours between connections, you may consider a layover to have lunch with a friend, schedule a business meeting, or plan a quick sight-seeing excursion. Instead of hanging around the airport, you can see a city you may want to visit later. How many times have you been stuck in the Denver, St. Louis, or Chicago airport? All major cities and their airports could use a "sight-seeing excursion introduction to our city" concept.

### ✈Travel Tip: Know Your Options

When you book your flight, either ask your travel agent or consult a flight schedule timetable to find out what other flights are going your way. Then, if your flight is canceled or delayed, you'll already know what choices you have. And when you check in for your flight, pick up one of the free flight schedules displayed on the counter of every ticket agent.

Barbara Sanfilippo, a speaker in the financial services industry, makes sure she is in control when flights are not on time. She says, "As soon as I get to the airport, I note if the plane is showing a delay. If so, I immediately call my travel agent and book an alternate flight. If my first flight is canceled or still delayed, I calmly go to the second gate and ask to be switched. Everyone else is sitting around or waiting in line."

Sanfilippo adds that if you really must get somewhere, book one ticket and double-book a back-up flight. (Of course, bad weather could cancel both.) Do not give your frequent flyer number at the time of the reservation. Then the airline cannot easily track your double-booking activities, which they frown upon (they may show their displeasure by canceling both flights). Remember to provide your frequent flyer number once you check in to your chosen flight, so you can get your points and preferred seat assignment.

If you travel often, consider subscribing to a flight schedule guide. A number of them list all the major airlines' flights, highlighting which is best for timing and connections. Access to all this information is on the Internet.

An alternative to these costly guides is to pick up the free system timetables from the airline you use most frequently.

## ✈Travel Tip: Call Again

If you book your flight directly with the airline, phone them a second time if you can't get what you want on the first call. Sometimes you can get what you want on the second call.

> *If you know it takes exactly 485 steps to walk from one end of the American Airlines concourse to the other at the Nashville airport, you've made connections there more than once. If you know you can save exactly 45 steps by taking the shortcut behind the Admirals Club at Gate 17, you spend as much time at the Nashville airport as you do at home.*
> 
> — Bryan Townsend

# Chapter 5
## Dr. Travel Prescribes: Choosing a Flight

## ✈Travel Tip: Book Off-Peak Flights and Less-Used Airports

- Avoid flying on a Friday. Instead, book your flight for a Tuesday or Wednesday, if you can. Midweek is less crowded.

- Avoid flights that depart or arrive between 7 to 9 A.M. and 4 to 7 P.M. at any major airport. These are the busiest times of the day. I know I said to take the earliest flights, but you should consider the length of the flight, how important your arrival time is for the trip, and the possibilities of being remanded to coach because you did not have seniority for the upgrade list.

- Consider using less crowded airports to major cities. For example, Hobby in Houston (instead of Houston International), Midway in Chicago (instead of O'Hare), Oakland in the San Francisco Bay Area (instead of San Francisco International), or Long Beach, Orange Country, or Burbank (instead of Los Angeles International).

## ✈Travel Tip: Know Your ABCs

Every airport has its own three-letter code. Some are easy to identify because they closely match the name of the city (like PIT for Pittsburgh or SFO for San Francisco. Others are more complicated (like MCO for Orlando or EWR for Newark).

If you travel regularly, it would pay you to know the airport codes. It can help you read your ticket more easily, keep track of your frequent flyer miles, and talk like an airport pro (that's PRO).

In addition to knowing the city codes, you should know a few acronyms:

ETA = Estimated time of arrival

ETD = Estimated time of departure

DT = Decision time (a determination of when a delayed flight might leave the gate)

Part I:
Get Ready for Take-Off

## ✈Travel Tip: Know Who's Late and Who's Not

Each month, the U.S. Department of Transportation (DOT) ranks the major airlines on their on-time records. The results are published in many newspapers. To increase your chances of being on time, consider booking your flight with the winner. *USA Today* publishes this information each month. In addition, the Internet now provides online information through DOT's home page, FAA, and each airline's Web site.

> *When a further delay was announced, I walked up to the ticket agent and said: "I don't see why you people bother publishing a flight schedule." The ticket agent replied in his usual calm, professional tone: "Well, Sir, we have to have something to base our delays on!"*
> — Joey Adams

## ✈Travel Tip: Know the Rules

Wise fliers know airline rules. So when things go wrong, they know the right way to deal with the problems

- Flight diverted?

Most carriers will let you make a short phone call or send a brief telegram at their expense. If it's mealtime, some will pay to feed you and some won't; ask for a meal voucher and see what they say. If you need to stay overnight because of a diversion, airlines usually put you up at a hotel (not your choice) and also pay for the hotel/airport ground transportation.

- Flight delayed?

Rolling delay: If your departure time is delayed because of mechanical reasons and the airlines announces a new departing time, and then keep advancing it (a *rolling delay*), inquire about being booked on the next flight or on another airline.

Weather delay: If the plane doesn't leave on time because of bad

# Chapter 5
## Dr. Travel Prescribes: Choosing a Flight

weather, you can't do much. All the airlines are in the same predicament. After they announce the new departure time, go for a walk or get a nosh.

- Why Are There Weather Delays in Good Weather?

*Case #1:* It's a perfectly sunny day. You have boarded your flight and are waiting on the tarmac to take off. Then the pilot announces your departure is no longer possible because of bad weather. How can this happen when it is a picture-perfect day outside the airplane window?

*Reason for delay:* The weather is terrible at your destination. The FAA (Federal Aviation Administration) insists pilots wait at the departure point to avoid air congestion at your destination.

*Case #2:* As in Case #1, the day is perfect and sunny. You are waiting to board your flight and the pilot announces your plane cannot leave due to bad weather. You wonder how can this happen when, outside the terminal, the weather is perfect!

*Reason for delay:* The weather is miserable at the airport from where your flight was to depart, so the flight is delayed.

As in the case of a plane being diverted, no matter what the cause, ask for either a meal voucher (if the delay is over four hours) or request a hotel voucher if you are away from home and it's past 10 p.m. Some airlines will give vouchers and some will not, but it never hurts to ask.

> *You're flying 500 mph, 30,000 feet in the air, and the pilot tells you to feel free to roam around the plane. But when you're on the ground taxiing to the gate at 1 mph, the pilot tells you to remain seated for your own safety.*
> — Elayne Boosler

- Flight canceled?

If your flight is canceled, the airline is responsible for getting you to your destination. The airlines will book you either on one of its other planes or on another carrier. The routing may vary from your original ticket but, eventually, you will get to where you are going. Sometimes, if the distance is not too great, the airline will bus you to your destination or to another airport.

Because airline cancellation policies differ from carrier to carrier, consult the conditions of carriage (the fine print contract) that accompanies your ticket.

- Bumped? (See Chapter 8)

On a domestic flight from Chicago to Cleveland, the flight continued to have a rolling delay. The flight attendant came through the cabin and gave out $25 discount coupons with no expiration date. Many passengers declined the offer (my take on the decline was an attempt at retribution for the delay). I thanked the flight attendant for her generosity, assured her I knew she was as much a victim as the passengers were, and offered to help her hand out the vouchers. She declined my offer, but returned later to hand me four dozen unclaimed discount coupons. "Here," she said, "thank you for offering to help and for being a gentleman." $1,200 worth of discount coupons. Not bad for being reasonable about a situation over which none of us had control. Later, as the flight finally landed, she again returned to give me a bottle of champagne from First Class. "Thanks again," she said. "Your offer to help stopped me from crying and making a fool out of myself. Please enjoy this champagne on me and the airline."

## ✈Travel Tip: Know Your Plane

- L-1011s have tiny overhead storage bins.
- 757s have one difficult-to-navigate, long, narrow aisle.

The exit row has the most legroom, as well as a wide distance from the back of the seat in front of you to your seat. This is my favorite seat so leave one for me.

- 737s generally have less legroom.

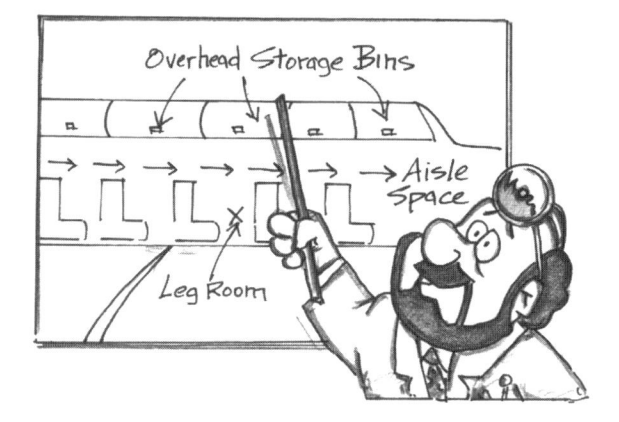

# Chapter 5
## Dr. Travel Prescribes: Choosing a Flight

- Both 737s and 757s have the fewest lavatories per capita.

- The most comfortable planes are 767s, 747s, MD-11s, and MD-80s.

- All lavatories are designed for people of below average height and weight. Go before you fly. If you can, wait until you land.

- Airlines change pillow cases only once or twice a day, even when a plane makes several flights. Pillow To Go® is a latex, foam rubber pillow for travelers that folds to 15" ( 13" to the size of a can of Pringles®.

> *Stranded at the airport when his plane was canceled, my brother Dennis was waiting with other disgruntled travelers for the next flight. Consulting a schedule, he mentioned to the man in front of him that phoning for a reservation would probably be the most efficient way to guarantee a seat. The man then proceeded to open his briefcase, produce a cellular phone, and book reservations for the two of them, to be picked up when they reached the counter.*
>
> — Dorothy Minette Gola

- Track your frequent flyer miles. Save receipts and boarding stubs until the flight is posted. MaxMiles is a softwear program that tallies miles earned in airline, hotel, and car rental programs. It will also track miles about to expire. The software is from Syphrosyny. You can find a demo version on the Web at http://www.maxmiles.com.

- Randy Petersen, editor of *Inside Flyer*, says frequent flyer miles can accumulate into a significant inheritance. All the airlines and hotels have rules on transfer to heirs, though. I suggest you give away mileage coupons to your family when you feel you cannot use them all to avoid any estate issues.

## ✈Travel Tip: Something Special in the Air

If you are looking for something different at 40,000 feet, you may want to fly on one of the following airlines:

- Virgin Atlantic Airways has massage therapists and manicurists for their Business Class customers on flights from New York to London.

- Japan Airlines offers Sky Massage, an in-flight automatic massage chair, to its First Class international passengers.

- Southwest Airlines holds in-flight contests. Sometimes prizes are given to passengers with the most credit cards in their wallet/purse, the biggest hole in their socks, or the ugliest photo on their driver's license. Another competition involves a flight attendant tossing a roll of toilet paper down the aisle. Winners are determined by where the roll stops.

- Singapore Airlines offers its First Class passengers personal foot massages, excellent food selections, and a choice of movies.

- United Airlines now offers individual video players with a large assortment of tapes for its First Class passengers, as well as the standard two or three movies on the larger screen.

> *Never . . . ever . . . fly on an airline that offers patio dining.*
>
> — Linda Perret

*Everything in airplanes has advanced except the seat you sit in.*

— *Condé Nast Traveler*

## Chapter 6
# Choosing a Seat

Airline seats are not designed to be occupied for long periods of time. Yet this is exactly what lengthy flights demand.

Some planes have more comfortable seating than others (the 767, for example, which is a bit roomier in coach), but most flatten the normal S curve of your spine. In addition, coach class seats have a limited *pitch* (the degree the seat will recline) and restrictive hip, elbow, leg, and derriere room.

The solution to this problem, of course, is to fly First or Business Class. Most of us, though, cannot afford the exorbitant extra cost for the limited extra comfort. Until the airlines correct the uncomfortable seating situation (probably on the 12th of Never), the answer to this dilemma is to make the best of a bad situation. Examine your personal preferences and in-flight habits and then select your place on the plane accordingly.

Mail-order catalog owner Lillian Vernon, says, "I like sitting by the window because I can nest there unbothered if I want to work. And the second row is far enough away from the food-service area that I'm not bothered by the noise if I want to sleep." Comedian Jay Leno, on the other hand, always sits in an aisle seat. "That way," he says, "I can be first out the door."

Taking another approach, celebrity chef Paul Prudhomme regularly requests the same seat. He finds sitting in the same place makes it easier to sleep because of the familiarity — like sleeping in your own bed.

Some road warriors have become so sophisticated in their selection of seats, they even think about which side of the plane to sit on. Author and seminar leader, T. Scott Gross from Texas, says he's right-handed, so he likes the left side of the aircraft because "it eliminates the shadow on my work."

A preference for an aisle, middle, or window seat, the front or rear of the aircraft, a bulkhead or exit row, the left or right side of the plane, is up to you. The following data may help you decide.

### Aisle Seat –
*Advantages:*
- Easy access both for bopping up and down to the restroom, (especially if you are going to drink lots of fluids, which is highly recommended) or in case of emergencies.
- Less claustrophobic than the center or wall/window seat.

*Disadvantages:*
- Drinks and ice are easily spilled on you.
- You will be bumped by the food and beverage carts or other passengers.
- Window and middle-seat passengers will climb over you.

> *1. No matter where you sit in an airplane, the person in the seat in front of you will recline the seat into your lap. 2. No matter where you sit in an airplane, the person in back of you will stick his or her feet against your elbow or stick his or her knees against the back seat. 3. No matter where you sit in an airplane, there will be, no further than three seats away, a woman with a hyper three-year-old child who will alternatively scream or throw food.*
>
> — C. R. Vest

# Chapter 6
## Dr. Travel Prescribes: Choosing a Seat

**Window Seat –**

*Advantages:*
- This is the best place to sleep. You have fewer people to annoy you and you can lean against the wall of the aircraft. If you want to sleep, make sure you sit away from the restrooms or galley.

- Best views. Daydream or write about the scenery below you. On one trip, for example with the help of Allan Klein, I wrote this after gazing out the window:

    > *Change is everywhere. Clouds move, sun breaks through, we are moving, the earth is moving, the universe is moving.*
    > — **Shi<sup>f</sup>t Happens!**®

*Disadvantages:*
- Less legroom because of the aircraft's curved side walls.
- You have to climb over people every time you want to get out.

**Front of Plane –**

*Advantages:*
- It saves time getting off the plane. And those few precious minutes can mean the difference between making or missing a close connection.

- Usually first to be served your meal and beverages.

- This is a bit quieter in coach. Fewer people pass by you on their way to the restroom or to find their friends.

- If you are worried about a fuel fire in the plane, sit forward of the wing. I sit in an exit row over the wing. The fuel is carried in the wings, so structurally this is the strongest part of the plane. In other words, the part that will break up last. In addition to sitting in the middle of the aircraft, I only have half the distance to travel forward or backward to another exit.

Part I:
Get Ready for Take-Off

*Disadvantage:*

- Last to board (unless you are in Business or First Class).

> *On some airlines the seats are very narrow. Turning the other cheek isn't a virtue, it's a necessity!*
> — Milton Berle

**Back of Plane –**

*Advantages:*

- First ones to board.
- First ones to get the coveted overhead bin spaces.
- Safer. Studies have shown that on most aircraft, the back third of the plane is safer than the front.
- Less crowded. Forward seats are more popular so they fill first. Also, many planes get narrower in the back so there are fewer people.
- If you are worried about impact (say, against the side of a mountain), these are the best seats.

*Disadvantages:*

- Takes longer to exit.
- Last row may not recline fully.
- Sometimes you are the last to be served your meal and beverages.
- Usually near the bathroom (this could be an advantage).

Charles Chittum, an expert at the world's foremost aircraft-crash survival program, the Federal Aviation Administration's Civil Aeromedical Institute in Oklahoma City, says the most important thing passengers can do is sit in their seats with their seat belts buckled. He suggests passengers leave seat belts on for the duration of the flight. Without seat belts in place, passengers run the risk of personal injury if the plane makes a sudden turn or the cabin experiences rapid decompression.

In addition to deciding on an aisle or window seat in the front or back of the aircraft, here are some other things that may make your flight more comfortable.

## ✈Travel Tip: Get an Advanced Seat Assignment

When you book your flight, ask for your seat preference. If you wait until you check-in at the airport, you are less likely to get the seat you want.

Most airlines, though, will not assign a seat more than 30 days before the flight. If you are a member of the airline's frequent flyer program, seat assignments, and even certain seats, are assignable well in advance as another perk for becoming an important customer.

> *A lady said she did not mind being put on standby for a flight. If they couldn't find her a seat, she would go to the gift shop and buy a little stool.*
> — Doc Blakely

## ✈Travel Tip: Request an Exit Row

On most airplanes, the spacing is wider in an exit row, so it usually has extra legroom. (On some planes, the seat next to the door has been removed, so you'll probably have more elbow room than legroom.)

In some planes, two exit rows are on each side of the plane, located over each wing. Make sure the arm rests are not stationary in the row you are assigned. What is the purpose of having the seat next to you empty if you can't use both seats? It could be quieter here, too. Federal regulations prohibit children under age fifteen in exit rows.

## Part I: Get Ready for Take-Off

On domestic flights, if you sit in an exit row, you must speak English and be able and willing to open the emergency door. You also will need to get to the airport early because airlines do not assign these seats in advance.

Al Walker, a motivational speaker, told me the following story: As a very large man, Walker often finds getting his seat belt to go around him difficult. He quietly asks the flight attendant for a seat belt extender. (This is the same device used in the preflight announcements to show you how to buckle your seat belt.) Often the flight attendants respect Walker's request and quietly and professionally deliver the extender, rolled up tightly. This is done with the same seriousness as if the attendant were informing a patient of a terminal illness. Other times, the extender is presented like a necktie, dangling from an outstretched arm with the announcement, "Here's your extender!"

On one flight, having survived the delivery of an extender without any announcement, Walker noticed another large man trying to get his seat belt fastened. The man's wife was lecturing him about losing weight. Walker began to tell the man about the extender, but stopped in mid-thought when the man looked at Walker, turned to his wife, and said, "I am not fat! If he can get that damn seat belt buckled, so can I!" At this point, the flight attendant stopped by Walker's seat and asked, "Shall we tell him about the extender?" She then answered her own question with, "No, I think we can let him suffer just a little more. How about after the preflight announcements?"

### ✈Travel Tip: Request a Bulkhead Seat ... Maybe

Bulkhead seats are immediately behind the partition that separates coach from the Business or First Class sessions. You have the advantage of having no seat in front of you that probably will recline and encroach on your already limited space. But beware, because of the divider, there may be less legroom.

The other disadvantage is you neither have storage under the seat in front of you for your carry-ons nor a seat pocket for your magazines and papers. (Bulkhead window seats, though, frequently have a pouch directly under the window.)

On most planes, if you take your shoes off, you can place your feet on the bulk head wall providing you with some additional legroom or a way to stretch out more comfortably.

One other small, but important, disadvantage of a bulkhead seat is the wall in front of you limits your field of vision, which can contribute to eye strain and fatigue.

> *Trying to get comfortable in an airline seat that — I think this has something to do with the Theory of Relativity — gets progressively smaller the farther the plane goes, so that by the middle of your second week en route (around hour 163 of the FAA-required In-Flight Movie That Nobody Ever Heard Of), your body has been compressed into a space the size of a gym locker, but somehow not as comfortable.*
> — Dave Barry

Most airlines reserve bulkhead seats for the physically challenged, families with infants, or unaccompanied minors, so they won't assign them until you check-in at the airport, unless, of course, you are a member of their high-volume frequent flyer program.

## ✈Travel Tip: Lift the Armrest

If the seat next to yours is empty, lift the armrest and stretch out. If the entire row is clear, you can even lift the armrests and lie down comfortably.

Comedian Paula Poundstone, in fact, prefers coach over First Class for this very reason. "I'm into coach because I like a row to myself, as opposed to sitting next to someone in First Class . . . the armrests don't go up in First Class and they do in coach."

Part I:
Get Ready for Take-Off

## ✈Travel Tip: When You "Vant to Be Alone"

- Ask for an aisle or a window seat. Middle seats fill up last.

- On wide-body aircraft, request an aisle seat in the center section. You'll have a better chance of having an empty seat next to you.

- When you check in for your flight, ask if the seat next to you is open. If it is not, request one that is open.

- When two people are traveling together on a plane with three-abreast seating, one person can request an aisle and the other person can request a window. This maximizes the chances of the seat in the middle remaining empty. (If someone does sit there and you want to sit next to your companion, you can ask the person to switch seats with either of you.) Look around for people who appear to be traveling together, but who did not get adjoining seat assignments. Offer to give up your seat, but make sure the flight attendant approves your request. Once you start to move, ask the flight attendant for another aisle seat. I have done this and have been upgraded because of my "good will gesture."

## Chapter 6
### Dr. Travel Prescribes: Choosing a Seat

## ✈Travel Tip: When Only Middle Seats Remain

- Ask the gate agent to put you between a couple on the flight. Often the one on the aisle will move in. (This is the reverse of the previous strategy.)

- Ask at the gate to be put on the wait-list for an aisle/window seat.

> *A young lady, who obviously had never been on a plane, was heard saying she didn't want to sit by a window because she didn't want to get her hair blown.*
> — Nancy and Dean Hoch, travel agents

- Take another flight. Once you have told the agent you cannot sit in a middle seat and will wait for the next flight, the agent will often find a seat that was blocked with no passenger checked in and he or she will release that seat to you. The ticket agent needs to board the flight with as many passengers as possible. Do not yell or chastise the agent. You will find yourself in the last seat, nearest the bathroom and galley. Be calm, respectful, and grateful!

## ✈Travel Tip: Upgrade Whenever You Can

Although the price of a First Class seat can cost as much as six times that of coach, ways exist to fly up front without setting you back too much.

Many airlines, for example, offer upgrades on a seat-available basis to their most frequent flyers. Upgrade coupons are usually bought, but are sometimes given away by the airline to encourage carrier loyalty. Frequent flier awards good for free flights can also be used to upgrade, but evaluate which is more valuable to you before you use them this way.

For less frequent fliers, some airlines sell Business or First Class seats at a small premium over coach. Ask your travel agent or air-

Part I:
Get Ready for Take-Off

line. Also, watch for airline ads that offer free companion tickets. Often two can fly in Business Class for little more than two coach tickets.

Try to get the flight attendant to upgrade you once you board the plane. This used to be easier than it is today due to the high number of upgrades required by the frequent flyer participants. Offer to have a coach meal. The airline may not have boarded extra First Class meals because the seats were empty.

## ✈Travel Tip: Play Musical Chairs

Just because you are assigned a seat, doesn't mean you have to sit in it. The moment the door of the plane is closed, seek out a more desirable seat and move to it. Make your move quickly, though. Others are making the same plans.

> *Please return your seat to its upright and most uncomfortable position. Later, you may lean back and break the knees of the passenger behind you.*
> — flight attendant

*Get out your scorecard, your calculator, and your damn minicomputer because that's what you'll have to have if you want the lowest fare.*
— Tom Parsons, Editor, *Best Fares*

## Chapter 7
# Cheap Travel

Once, when I was booking a flight, I glanced at the reservation screen. I was amazed to find 40 different fares were available for the same flight. Much depended on when I wanted to go, how soon ahead I'd be ticketing, and a host of other factors too involved for me to comprehend. From that day on, I have stopped booking my own flights using a computer. I now understand the rules, have definite goals, and fully expect the airline or travel agent to give me all the options, including those I know they will not tell me until I ask.

Part I:
Get Ready for Take-Off

Finding the cheapest airfare is often a combination of flexibility, timing, and luck. That's where a good travel agent can be helpful. But the airlines have so many special promotions, discounts, and fare wars, you might frequently hear about them even before your agent does. Be an informed consumer.

In a recent *20/20* television program (5/25/98), Barbra Walters and Arnold Diaz of *ABC News* discussed airline fares with Terry Trippler, editor, *Airfare Report.com*. *NBC Nightly News* also had a feature on the high cost of airline tickets the same week. The following information is based on those two broadcast reports.

Here are the twelve ways to get the lowest fare when the airlines are having specials . . . and even when they're not.

- **The Weekend Stay-Over**

Because the airlines know business travelers generally cannot stay over a weekend, the cost of a mid-week fare is significantly higher than one that includes a Saturday night. Sometimes the difference can be double the price.

So, if you are looking for a lower fare, make sure it includes a Saturday night (for example, departing on a Tuesday and returning the following Monday).

- **The One-Stop**

A flight that makes a stop between your departure city and your destination can sometimes be significantly cheaper than one that makes no stops. Although you might have to spend an extra hour or two on the ground, and you risk additional delays, the savings may be worth it.

> *The Lord must have loved airline fares. He made so many of them.*
> — Milton Berle

# Chapter 7
## Dr. Travel Prescribes: Cheap Travel

- **The Fare Wars**

Perhaps the lowest fares you can get (not counting using your frequent flier miles for a free trip) is when the airlines have a fare war or airfare sale. To get these:

- Check your newspaper daily for bargain fares.

- Check the Internet. Airlines now use this distribution channel to provide low fares without advising travel agents.

- Immediately call either the airline or your travel agent (seats are limited and go quickly). Look before you book, though. Sometimes the competition will come up with a sweeter deal.

- Keep trying if you can't get through right away.

- When you do reach the reservation agent, be as flexible as possible about your date and time of departure.

- Often the competition will match another airline's fares even if they haven't had time to advertise it. Call to find out.

- Don't assume the fare war is over on the date advertised; sometimes there are unadvertised extensions.

- Read the small print. The fares listed are usually one-way (even though you have to buy a round trip), and they come with restrictions (such as, you must stay over a Saturday night or travel only on a Tuesday or Wednesday). Although the ticket may be nonrefundable, you can usually change flights for a small additional fee. The catch is if no more discounted fares exist, you may have to pay this fee plus the difference between your original fare and your re-booked fare.

*If an ad seems too good to be true, it probably is.*
– Cornish Hitchcock,
Aviation Consumer Action Project

- **The Split**

First find out what it would cost to fly nonstop from your originating city to your destination — for instance, Los Angeles to Dallas. Then call back and inquire what it would cost to fly from Los Angeles to Albuquerque and then fly from Albuquerque to Dallas. Sometimes splitting the fare, by buying two tickets, is cheaper than buying one ticket for the nonstop.

The drawbacks: you can't check your Los Angeles luggage through to Dallas. And the airlines are not responsible if you miss your connection in Albuquerque.

- **The Throw-Away**

Because flights that involve a weekend stay-over are less expensive than those that don't, on some routes it is cheaper to buy two round-trips and to throw away half of each. For example, suppose you want to fly from San Francisco to Chicago on a Wednesday and return Friday of the same week. Book one flight with the outbound trip on Wednesday and the return portion for any day the following week. Book another ticket from Chicago to San Francisco on the Friday you want, with the return portion from San Francisco to Chicago also the following week.

Both tickets now have a weekend stay-over. You only use the first part of each ticket and throw away the second. You travel on the days you want, you don't stay over a weekend, and you save a bundle. (If you travel the same route regularly, this strategy is even more useful. Instead of throwing away the second half of the ticket, use it for another trip.)

Airlines hate throw aways. They believe throwaways are a violation of their right to overcharge their business passengers. One major airline in the Twin Cities now cancels the second ticket if they catch some one using throw aways on their airline. My suggestion is to purchase tickets as previously described, but to use two different airlines. This makes it difficult for the airline to find out you are using throw aways.

# Chapter 7
## Dr. Travel Prescribes: Cheap Travel

*There are no two people on an airplane who have paid the same price for a seat. Think about it and it will make you crazy. Some are relatives of airline employees who pay nothing, Some are traveling on amassed mileage coupons, and some are on super savers where they travel on Tuesday morning only during the months when oysters are in season if they buy their tickets at high tide on the day they were born.*

— Erma Bombeck

- **The Advance Purchase**

Unless the airlines are having some kind of special promotion, the closer you book your ticket to your departure date, the more you will pay. Try to ticket at least two to three weeks (fourteen to twenty-one days) before you travel for the best deals.

- **The Double-Overlapping-Open-Jaw**

No, this is not a special fare for people who have just had dental work. It is a way of booking a ticket for midweek flights to multiple cities without paying the higher midweek fares.

This is similar to throw-away ticketing, where you book your return for a latter date so it includes a weekend stay-over, even though you don't actually stay over a Saturday night. The difference is this ticketing involves more than two cities.

For example: On April 3, you want to go from Chicago (ORD) to Fort Lauderdale (FLL) and return on April 6. Then on April 18, you need to make a trip from Chicago (ORD) to Atlanta (ALT) and return on April 21.

Typically, you would book one ticket this way:
April 3 ORD FLL
April 6 FLL ORD

And the second trip this way:
April 18 ORD ALT
April 21 ALT ORD

Part I:
Get Ready for Take-Off

Both trips are midweek and very expensive. So instead book it this way:
April 3 ORD  FLL
April 21 ALT  ORD

And the second trip this way:
April 6 FLL  ORD
April 18 ORD ATL

On your first trip, use the ORD/FLL coupon on the first ticket for your outbound flight. For the return, use the first coupon on your second ticket, FFL/ORD.

On your second trip, use the remaining coupon on your second ticket for your outbound flights, ORD/ATL. For the return, use the remaining coupon on your first ticket, ATL/ORD.

Booking this way gives you the lower Saturday night stay-over fare and you don't stay over the weekend.

To book this kind of ticket, the surface leg (Fort Lauderdale/Atlanta) must be shorter than the flight and, for the most savings, ticket at least two weeks in advance.

> No wonder tickets are expensive. According to a research firm in VA, flying B747's costs $2,600/hour in fuel, $800/hour in crew, $1,400/hour in total maintenance.
> — *Travel Smart* newsletter

- **The Buy and Fly**

A number of household products occasionally have coupons attached that offer discounted airline tickets. In the past, several cereals had twenty-five percent off coupons for flights on one airline, while a nationally known mail-order catalog offered upgrades if you purchased something from them.

Sometimes it is the airlines themselves who offer promotional

Chapter 7
Dr. Travel Prescribes: Cheap Travel

discount coupons in newspapers or to their frequent fliers. If you want to use the coupon on a different airline than the one that issued it — ask! They may accept it.

> *It was bound to happen. Airline fares have become so complicated, it's now cheaper to fly to some destinations than to stay home.*
> — Gary Apple

- **The Unconventional**

Airlines frequently run special promotions.

One airline had low-fare one-day-only excursions to Minnesota's Mall of America and another had special Elvis fares. For the latter, you had to fly to and from Memphis, Presley's home town, on the date of his birth, January 8. Another airline topped this deal and offered a $20 refund if passengers showed up at the gate dressed like Elvis.

One carrier, playing around with the connection between airlines and peanuts, offered two-for-one fares to customers who took peanuts to the ticket counters.

Granted these fares are limited and restrictive (and they could cost you more than you would save if you don't own an Elvis costume). Nevertheless, bargain fares can be found if they meet your needs.

- **The Close-Enough**

Sometimes flying to a near-by city is less expensive than flying to your final destination. You might, for example, fly to Milwaukee instead of Chicago, to Omaha instead of Lincoln, or, Long Beach instead of Los Angeles.

Of course, if you have to rent a car, the savings might be a washout.

Part I:
Get Ready for Take-Off

- **The Hidden-City**

Sometimes you can get to where you want to go by pretending to fly somewhere else — *hidden city ticketing.*

Say you want to go from Seattle to Dallas, but the fare is exorbitant. But a much lower promotional fare is on flights from Seattle to Miami with one stop in Dallas. You book that one and get off the plane in Dallas. (Naturally, you can't check any bags or they will go to Miami.)

One major problem with hidden-city ticketing is it's against airline regulations (so most travel agents won't do it, you must book it yourself).

The other difficulty is you can't buy a round-trip ticket — the airline will cancel the return segment. But you can buy another one-way ticket back to the original city. If you do, route it differently than the first ticket and do so only after the first ticket has been used. Or, use another carrier. Airlines do not share ticketing information. Do not use your frequent flyer number when you book the tickets. Offer that number only when you check-in at the airport.

Some people are using this, as one magazine called it, "tricky-ticketing-tactic" to save money. But beware, it's risky.

*"High Season" begins the day you need to travel.*
*— Travel Smart newsletter*

- **The Special Fare**

Most airlines offer some sort of special fare for college students and for senior citizens. The "senior" age range differs slightly, however, so check your carrier. If you qualify, you'll get ten percent off on most airlines. In addition, senior citizens can purchase deep-discount coupon books.

Although it's not a fare you will use often, if you have had a death in your family and you need to travel to the funeral, ask the airline about its bereavement fare. Many offer a fifty percent reduction off their full-fare ticket. However, you do need proof to get this discount.

## ✈Travel Tip: Fare Warning

The ticket must be in your name. If it's in someone else's name, the airlines have a right to deny you boarding.

## ✈Travel Tip: Best Fares

*Best Fares* is one of the best magazines in the country, and it works for the passenger, not for the travel industry. Hidden-fare cities, promotional fares, special frequent flyer offers, hotel discounts and more make this a subscription well worth its cost(s).

To order call *Best Fares* at 800-880-1234 or visit them at http://www.bestfares.com. They also offer several travel clubs including air, hotel, and cruise. Tell them Dr. Travel sent you and ask for their special offer.

Part I:
Get Ready for Take-Off

*Enter the consolidator, which sells discounted airline tickets like a fashion outlet store sells discount clothes. Both may hide the brand name, restrict charge cards, and refuse refunds.*

— Cathy Lynn Grossman

## Chapter 8
# Cheaper Travel

Greenair, an airline carrier in Turkey, once offered half fares to green-eyed women. This section will show you how to seek out deeply discounted or free fares . . . and you needn't reside in Turkey, be female, or have green eyes.

## Consolidators

Consolidators buy blocks of tickets from the airlines and resell them to the public — either directly or through travel agencies — at a discount. While these consolidators may save you hundreds of dollars, caution should be taken when you deal with them.

- During fare wars, consolidators may not offer the lowest prices. Compare their price with the airline's deal.

- Discount agencies frequently can't deliver on the fares they advertise.

- Only use a discounter who will accept a credit card payment. If they don't deliver, cancel the charge.

- If the consolidator can't guarantee a firm reservation, don't pay in advance. In addition, the reservation should be on the airline's computer by the following day.

- Ask about the consolidator's cancellation/refund policy.

- Ask if you can get frequent flier miles, special meals, or advanced seat selection. Often you can't.

- You are limited to international flights. Most consolidators don't deal with domestic travel.

> *Frequent flier miles are a brilliant idea. If you travel all the time for a living and build up thousands of miles, you get a free trip. This is just what people who travel all the time want to do on their time off. It's like giving a trash collector who finished a thousand runs a free ride on the truck.*
> — Rita Rudner

## Frequent Flier Tickets

"There is a story," reported *Inside Flyer* magazine, "about a corpse that received frequent flyer miles, when it was flown home for burial. It seems that the man's widow had his frequent flyer card taped to the coffin . . . and the airline honored the request."

The next time you do some flying (hopefully, while you're alive), make sure you belong to that carrier's frequent flier program. Even if you never set foot on a plane again, you might earn a free flight. Airlines now give mileage credit for all kinds of things — for joining, for credit card purchases, for filling out surveys, for making phones calls, for buying flowers, mortgages, buying and selling stocks, and more.

Two other money-related reasons exist why it makes sense to join frequent flier programs — it doesn't cost anything and the airlines sometimes run members-only promotional specials.

Here are a few key opportunities and how to take advantage of them.

- *Airline/Hotel Anniversaries.* Each offers special deals to their frequent plan members. This information is provided in the monthly statements.
- *Internet.* Special offers are frequently valid only for a short

# Chapter 8
## Dr. Travel Prescribes: Cheaper Travel

period of time or over the upcoming weekend, but they do offer wonderful savings. Call the airlines or surf the Web for the name of the Web sites that correspond to the airlines flying to your destination.

- *Partnerships.* Free tickets are not the best use of your miles. Certainly purchasing upgrade certificates is not. Check to see if your miles can be used to purchase merchandise, lodging, cruises, or other items that may have a higher "net" cost to you. Consider using the miles to cut the cost of renting a car, purchasing theater tickets, or skiing in Vail. American Airlines offers redemption at both major hotels and car-rental firms.

**In my opinion, Diners Club is the best program.** You accumulate two points per dollar. The points are convertible for airline programs or you can purchase merchandise, hotels, cruises, wine, food, or even donate the value to charity. If you reach a high level of points (currently 250,000) you can request their concierge service. This means you can order anything (and I mean anything) you want. The laptop I am using to write this book is compliments of Diners Club.

- *Shop around.* If you belong to more than one frequent flyer program, compare costs. Look at each statement brochure so you can see what is available. Always make sure you include ALL your frequent flyer numbers when you travel. On many flights, I charge the ticket on Diners Club, which also provides insurance, then get miles from the airline, charge my hotel stay with their cobranded VISA or Mastercard so I get double points (i.e., Marriott) and pay the car rental with frequent flyer certificates so that is free.

- *Last minute frequent flyer seats.* Airlines have a huge debt to pay off with the millions of frequent miles accumulated by their passengers. They started to date the miles so expiration would assist in reducing the liability. In addition, they have become more willing to offer seats on selected flights that

Part I:
Get Ready for Take-Off

may have been designated for paying customers. Call the airline every two weeks prior to ten days before you want to travel. Many of the seats get released ten days prior to the flight. If you are willing to risk wait until the last minute you might, be rewarded.

Double-book the flight to make sure. In other words, book a normal reservation and do NOT provide your frequent flyer number. Use initials or a slight name alteration like Doc Travel instead of Doctor. Once you get the last minute deal, make sure you cancel the reservation. Airlines do not like this procedure, but then we do not like many of their policies. I guess it is just how to play the game. Remember, if they catch you they may cancel any flight that has not been ticketed.

## Travel Secret: Get More Value by Not Using Your Frequent Flyer Miles to Obtain Your Ticket

You may get more value by using the miles to purchase a hotel night or a merchandise item. Find out the number of miles needed for a ticket, or airline upgrade package and the price if you paid cash. Divide the miles into the quoted price and you will obtain the value, per mile, the airline is offering. The only time that I use frequent flyer points to purchase an airline ticket is for a trip with little or no advance notice, mid-week, with no Saturday stay. Those tickets are always very costly. Now the airlines do not even provide large discounts for bereavement trips. Save those miles but do not let them expire.

## Travel Secret: Nonstop Way to Free Flights

- Stick with one airline to build up mileage as quickly as possible. (Another reason to accumulate mileage on one carrier is once you reach a certain level of actual miles flown within a year, you get preferential treatment — everything from separate check-in lines to upgraded seating.)
- Choose a carrier whose hub is nearest your home because

that carrier will probably have the heaviest schedule from that city. Or, if you fly to the same destination a lot, stick with that carrier to rake up frequent flier miles.

- If you have the time and you are trying to accumulate as many miles as possible, book connecting flights rather than nonstops. You get credit for each leg of the trip.

> *Frequent flier miles have become the new global currency*
> — Randy Petersen,
> editor, *Inside Flyer*

- Get an airline-affiliated credit card. Then everything you charge (including airline tickets) will rack up mileage. (The banks usually assess an annual fee for these cards, so make sure you charge enough on them to get at least one free trip (about 25,000 dollars per year = one free domestic ticket.)

## Travel Secret: Once You Join, Keep Track of Your Mileage

- In many programs, miles expire if not used within a certain period of time.

- Carry a photo I.D. Airlines require it on frequent flier award tickets to prevent passengers from reselling them.

- Buying, selling, or bartering awards is illegal. You can, however, give them to others. Check with the individual airline to find out if that person must be a relative.

- Be aware that tickets obtained through frequent flier miles do not get the same treatment as paying passengers if there is a delay or cancellation. The airlines are less likely to endorse it over to another carrier and you might not receive hotel or food vouchers if you're stranded overnight.

Part I:
Get Ready for Take-Off

## Bumping

One way to obtain a ticket without paying for it is to volunteer to give up your seat (to be *bumped*) when flights are sold out. Since airlines often overbook to make up for people who do not show up, this option arises frequently.

If you volunteer to go on a later flight, the airlines can offer you anything — from a voucher for a future flight to extra frequent flier miles. The more seats needed and the fewer passengers willing to give them up, the better your chance of negotiating for a larger compensation — try, for example, for an extra travel voucher.

If you are involuntarily bumped, the airlines are more apt to stick to the rules set by the U.S. Department of Transportation:

- You get nothing if your originally scheduled plane is switched to a smaller aircraft, or if your aircraft carries fewer than sixty passengers.

- You are not entitled to any compensation if you are rebooked and you can reach your destination within an hour of your original flight.

- If the airline cannot get you to your destination within two hours of your original scheduled arrival time, they must pay you $200 (for domestic flights), or the one-way fare, whichever is less. If it's over two hours, the price doubles to $400, or the one-way fare, whichever is less. In addition, the airline will fly you to your destination free and you will keep your original ticket.

*My kids tease me. They say that I'm the first to get to the airport to volunteer to not get on the plane.*
— Stephen Forsyth,
President, *Forsyth Travel Library*

84

Chapter 8
Dr. Travel Prescribes: Cheaper Travel

## Travel Secret: If You Don't Want to be Bumped

- Get to the gate *at least* twenty to thirty minutes before departure.
- When a flight is oversold and no passengers have volunteered to be bumped, the last ones to check-in are the first to be denied boarding. Remember, many airlines now require check-in at least twenty minutes before the flight leaves.

## Travel Secret: If You Want to Be Bumped

- When you check in, let the gate agent know you are willing to give up your seat if needed.

> *My brother is a very serious, dignified man, so his actions one time at the airport's check-in counter were totally unexpected. It seems that he and his wife were placing their baggage on the conveyor when my sister-in-law's purse accidentally fell onto the moving belt. She scrambled after it but it eluded her, so she climbed onto the belt to try to reach it. Just as she was about to disappear through the doorway with the baggage, my brother began to wave frantically. "No, no, dear!" he shouted. "It's okay! This time we bought tickets."*
> — Carole Pratt

## Travel Secret: Before You Take the Ticket and Run

- Find out how long you have to wait for the next flight to your destination.
- Ask if you can get a confirmed reservation on that flight.
- Determine whether

Part I:
Get Ready for Take-Off

the money offered will cover hotel, meals and ground transportation costs that you might incur.

- Inquire if the airline will pay for meals and a hotel if you are stranded overnight.
- Check if any restrictions are on the travel voucher you will receive.
- While you're querying, also ask if you can be upgraded to First or Business Class on the rebooked flight. Sometimes airlines will do this.

## The Startups

When a small airline first starts flying, it usually offer low introductory fares to get your business. Generally these companies are not on your travel agent's computer reservation system, so you will have to search them out yourself.

Similarly, when the "grown-up" airlines open a new route they frequently offer lower fares in that market. Those can be booked through a travel agent.

> *It was a no-frills airline. Before the flight, the captain asked the passengers to chip in for gas!*
> — Milton Berle

## Courier Travel

Because shipping items overseas by freight is more expensive and time-consuming that shipping them as checked baggage, companies sometimes hire couriers to accompany the shipment. Although couriers must pay a fee, it is often less than half the cheapest round-trip advance-purchase fare. The significant saving, however, does come with drawbacks:

- You must travel alone.

- You are only allowed one carry-on.
- You can only stay at your destination a limited number of days.
- There is no demand for couriers for domestic travel.

## Travel Secret: No Matter What You Pay

- Keep rechecking your airfare. If it goes down before you fly, airlines will often refund the difference. However, they now charge $50–$75 to reissue a ticket. Make sure you can save more than it costs you.
- Use a credit card to purchase your tickets. If the airline goes under, you are more likely to get a refund.
- No matter what you pay, ask: "Is there anything cheaper if I leave at another time or on another day?"
- If you want to upgrade airline seating using frequent flyer miles, your best chance is to fly on Saturday or Sunday. Business travel is heaviest on Wednesday, Thursday, and Friday. Check with the airline for deviations to this pattern to Las Vegas, Washington, D.C., and other airports that do not conform to the normal arrival and departure patterns of the rest of the county.
- Never accept the first offer — **Never!**

Recently I had to fly from Chicago to Washington, D.C. I called eighteen days prior to the travel date but I did not meet the Saturday night stay requirement. This trip was just an overnight trip. I was quoted $1,345. I then said I could go into either Dulles or National and I could leave at any time during the day. I was given three choices of departure times, arriving at National instead of Dulles, and a rate of $149. And because I was a premier frequent flyer, I was upgraded to First Class for less than $50 in frequent flyer coupons.

Part I:
Get Ready for Take-Off

## Chapter 9
# Why Do You Think They Call It "Luggage"?

Robin Leach, host of *Lifestyles of the Rich and Famous,* lives out of a suitcase 300 days a year. He travels with seventy pieces of luggage. The next two chapters show you how to take sixty-nine suitcases fewer than Leach, how to select a suitcase, and what things to pack that you may not have considered.

### Making a Case for the Suitcase

A vast variety of luggage choices exists. To find the type that suits you best, consider:

- How much does the bag weigh empty?
- How much will you be using it — once a week or once a year?
- How much will you be packing — overnight clothes or a set of law books?
- Will you be using the suitcase for business or pleasure? Or both?
- How will you carry the suitcase — by the handle, on your shoulder, or by its wheels?
- Soft-sided versus hard? Soft is lighter, but easier to damage; hard is heavier, but it holds up better to baggage smashers. (If you purchase soft-sided, make sure it has reinforced corners.)

Part I:
Get Ready for Take-Off

- Expensive versus inexpensive? Expensive is more apt to be stolen. Cheap falls apart sooner.
- One-compartment versus multicompartment bag? Non-sectioned enables you to put things where you want. Sectioned keeps belongings separate and in place.

  > *It's just an observation, but handlers throw tapestried luggage harder — and don't catch it.*
  > — Hal Rubenstein and Jim Mullen

- Garment bag or regular? Garment bags are great if you can hang them up. Most aircraft, however, have little or no closet space to stow them (unless you are in First Class, and even then there's limited room on smaller aircraft).
- Samsonite™ is the choice of four out of ten travel agents. First choice of flight attendants/pilots is Travelpro™ from Eiffel™. And as I previously mentioned, Travelpro™ now makes a Platinum version that has heavier wheels, stronger pull handles, and reinforced zippers, corners, and inside pockets.
- Mulholland Brothers is my personal choice for several of their bags, including their safari bags. Their safari bag and I have traveled hundreds of thousands of miles. It opens from the top like the old doctor's bag. It has straps on each side to hold an overstuff bag, as well as a locking center strap. The bag comes with an over-the-shoulder strap, so I have a choice of how to carry it . . . using the handles or the strap. I am often stopped in the airport to provide information about the bag. This bag is manufactured with several types of materials, including leather and a combination of canvas and leather. After hundreds of flights, this bag still looks like the day I bought it, except it is now softer and has a golden hue. For more information, look at my resource center in the back of this book.

Chapter 9
Dr. Travel Prescribes: Why Do You Think They Call it "Luggage"?

## Luggage carts

If your luggage does not have built-in wheels (highly recommended), then consider getting a luggage cart. Consider these pluses and minuses when traveling with one:

*Advantages:*
- You no longer need to carry heavy items.
- You can carry your luggage and all the other materials you needed for the trip without a skycap.
- Luggage carts are great for several pieces of luggage, with or without wheels, because one person can manage all the bags while the others attend to picking up the rental car, calling the hotel, and so forth.

*Disadvantages:*
- Another thing to carry.
- Must be assembled and disassembled when getting on/off the plane.
- Cannot be stored in the overhead bin; must fit under your seat.
- Not designed for those without upper body strength.
- Not designed for those with designer fingernails.
- Not designed by designers who actually had to carry the cart, hold a briefcase, and search for airline tickets.

> *Things you'll never hear when you are traveling: Wait. Your suitcase looks a little damaged. Let me give you a new one.*
>
> — David Brenner

Part I:
Get Ready for Take-Off

## Travel Secret: Become a Member of the Tag Team

- Use luggage tags but avoid any that might suggest affluence. AAA suggests putting your business address on your luggage tags; a home address may suggest to potential thieves that your house will be vacant.

- In addition to luggage tags, make sure to put your name, address, and telephone number inside your luggage.

- Also, put the dates of your stay and where you want lost luggage to be delivered in the city you're visiting. John Jay Daly, president of Daly Communication, in Chevy Chase, Maryland, says, "I've only needed this one time but that's all it takes. And this was a Manhattan cabbie who carted the suitcase to the 12th floor Board Room I was conferring in . . . all because the outside of my case had my itinerary on it."

> *The type of luggage you carry says a lot about you. For example, if you're carrying somebody else's luggage, it says you're a thief.*
> — Dave Barry

## Travel Secret: For Safety Sake

- Make your luggage look different. Bags frequently go astray because they look like someone else's and someone walks off with one that looks like yours. You can consider buying bright-colored luggage, putting a colorful luggage strap around your bag or, using DayGlo stickers to make your suitcase stand out in a crowd. Brightly colored luggage also makes your bag a less-likely candidate for theft.

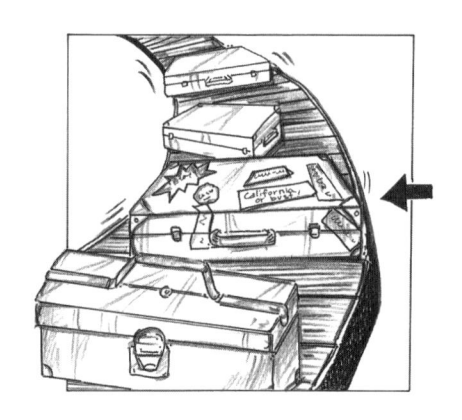

# Chapter 9
## Dr. Travel Prescribes: Why Do You Think They Call it "Luggage"?

- After your flight lands, pick-up your luggage as soon as possible. Items left circling on the baggage carousel can go astray.

  *Anyone traveling with obviously valuable baggage might as well post a "steal me" sticker on it.*
  — *Consumer Reports* Travel Letter

- Lock your bags. No guarantee exists that a lock will keep the contents safe, but a good lock is a good deterrent against thieves. I always carry plastic cable locks in my luggage. Available at any large hardware store, these ties have teeth on one end, so when you insert one end into the other, the tie is *locked* together. The only way to remove the plastic tie is to cut it off. While these ties do not prevent a thief from opening your bag, they do give you an instant indication someone has broken into your luggage. The plastic tie also guarantees the zipper on your bag remains closed if the lock is caught on the conveyor belt. Send your address to our Web site (http://www.doctor-travel.com) and I will send you a set of cable locks.

- Use luggage straps. Luggage straps are another hindrance against pilferage and insurance for faulty locks.

  *Be honest. When you signed up for a trekking vacation, did you ever expect to pay $1,000 a week for accommodations where the adjoining bathroom is a bush?*
  — Bob Baseman

## Travel Tip: Some Packing Tips

- Save your dry cleaner's bags. Clothes packed in plastic move around and don't wrinkle easily.

- Don't pack all your clothes in one bag, especially if you are traveling with someone else. Pack some of your clothes in your travelling companion's bag and have him or her pack some clothes in your bag. If luggage is lost neither of you will be without clothes. Remember, the airlines normally find a

Part I:
Get Ready for Take-Off

bag within 24 hours. Hotels and cruise ships don't have the same track record. Often the bag is sitting in someone's room — unnoticed — until it's time to leave. Only then is the bag discovered. If you have checked out previously, you may never see your bag, or its contents, again. Make sure a phone number is listed on the outside luggage tag.

- Use lots of Ziploc® bags when you pack. Organize your clothes. Use the bags to preven wrinkles. Carry small repair items, extra dental floss, and change inside your carry-on, so you can find it easily. I keep one just for receipts, another for calling cards, and a third for menu or other items I want to save from the trip.

- Take your medicine with you on the plane. Do not check medicine. Don't pack any items you may need within 24 hours. Never leave tickets, passports, visas, prescriptions, or other important items inside your luggage. Also, remember the inside of the airline or cruise cabin may get hot in the summer. Keep your cosmetics cool or you will find a lipstick popsicle. You can usually replace anyting you forgot. Enjoy your trip and don't sweat the small stuff.

Question: Where does all the lost luggage go?

Answer: Scottsboro, Alabama.

Want an inexpensive wedding ring? A set of second-hand crutches? A hardly used hearing aid? Then get yourself to Alabama. Three unclaimed baggage centers there sell all that unclaimed baggage "stuff."

*I have been to almost as many places as my luggage.*
— Bob Hope

*Why do I need so much luggage? Because foreign countries are all out of town. And I won't know what I need until I get there.*

— Gracie Allen

## Chapter 10
# Wheels of Fortune

Before you can take a trip, the first step is to pack. But you can't pack if you have no luggage. I'm amazed at how many people borrow luggage, purchase whatever is on sale, or use worn luggage that may not last the entire trip. In many cases, travelers plan their trip with great precision, except when they make one of the most important decisions of any trip. Nothing ruins a trip more than arriving at a destination without your luggage — nothing! You feel empty and violated. You talk to yourself and ask "Why me?" Who do you complain to at the airline? This chapter concerns itself with, not what or how to pack, but what to pack in: luggage.

Hundreds of luggage manufacturers exist worldwide. Each provides dozens of types of luggage in many colors and materials. *Nested bags,* one large bag with a smaller bag inside containing another smaller bag, can be purchased at discount stores and garage sales. Designer luggage from Louis Vitton, Hermes, and Ralph Lauren are normally sold in stores bearing their names. The rest of the luggage is available to all of us through normal retail stores, specialty stores, mail order and on the internet. Before making any purchase decision, I suggest the following:

1. Look at what kind of luggage others use. You can see suit–

Part I:
Get Ready for Take-Off

cases at an airport or in a hotel lobby, Hundreds of bags await distribution at cruise terminals and on luggage carousels at the airports.

2. Estimate your requirements. How often will you travel in the next year? How many times will your luggage be transported by airlines, cruises, or hotel personnel? Will you carry this bag yourself or check it most of the time? Do you drive yourself to the airport, have someone else drive you, or take public transportation?

3. Read ads. Visit specialty luggage stores. Ask questions. Explain the nature of your trip. For example, if you take a cruise, you will empty the bag at the start of the cruise and never look at it again until you repack for the trip home. On a hiking trip, you may have to backpack your belongings. In each case, your clothes should arrive safely at your destination.

4. Compare quality, price, style, convenience, and match them to your personal taste. Make sure you are objective in your assessments. How will you carry the bag: will you pull it, push it, put it over your shoulder, or strap it across your back?

5. Ask others about their luggage when you travel. For some reason, travelers like to talk about their favorite luggage as if it were a member of the family.

6. Evaluate durability, ease of packing, strength of handles and straps, reliability of wheels, and resistance to damage by the various handlers throughout your trip. You may not have your luggage at all times. Make sure the handles and straps are comfortable and well-anchored. All the stitching should be triple-stitched and, if possible, riveted to add additional security at stress points. For example, the Hartmann Fold Over/Four-Suiter has two leather straps on each side to close the bag. Hartmann tried to save money by using a thick piece of leather for the bottom strap but used a lightweight piece of leather for the top strap. Because the top strap is the

one that has the least amount of pressure, Hartmann assumed needn't be as strong. They were wrong. I have replaced the top strap on the bag three times in the last two years. Hartmann does send me a replacement, at no charge, but it still takes time to replace the straps.

*I go to encounter the reality of experience.*
— James Joyce

Luggage may be classified as follows:
- ✓ Bags you use for the day
- ✓ Bags you use for business trip
- ✓ Bags you take on vacation

## Bags you use for the day

***Tote bags.*** These are usually nonstructured with a large opening at the top. I prefer bags with a leakproof lining. Mesh or zippered pockets on the outside of the bag are handy for those items you may need (then you don't need to empty the contents of the entire bag when you search for something). My first choice is a bag with zippered pockets on the inside, as well as the outside. Also make sure the strap allows for easy hanging of a full bag from your shoulder.

***Gym bags.*** How can today's traveler, serious about fitness, not have a bag specifically designed for the gym all packed and ready to go? The lighter, the more pockets (mesh and closed), and waterproof and dry sides make this bag second only to the briefcase as the most replicated bag in luggage history. Not to be confused with

Part I:
Get Ready for Take-Off

other mesh bags, such as a beach bag or open tote, the gym bag is designed to hold shoes, damp swimsuits, and toiletries. Both hand and shoulder straps are included, but no lock is ever provided.

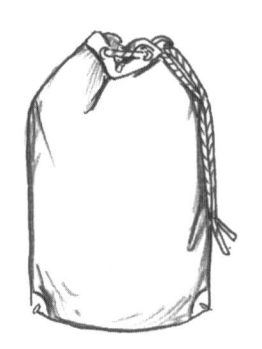

**Single purpose bags.** Remember your first sleep over? You probably used the laundry bag or pillow case. You stuffed in your jammies, toothbrush, flashlight, and either your teen magazine or comic books. Remember not to pack more than you need or more than you can lift.

**Beach bags.** Enough said.

**Overnight bags.** These have a large opening at the top. No need for a lock because you won't let this bag out of your sight. Nylon or canvas can be washed clean. Leather is heavier and it ages so the color will tell others the bag has been around. Think of a large grocery bag with handles. Think of a gym bag without lots of pockets or compartments. In each case, you can overstuff the bag with clothes you"ll wear the next day. In most cases, you will be at your destination in a short time and you can hang up your clothes.

Packing in plastic or between tissue paper reduces the wrinkles so you needn't spend your entire overnight ironing your clothes.

## Bags you use for a business trip

**Brief case.** Because the brief case is the preeminent piece of luggage for all business persons, I feel compelled to include it here. Most of the luggage manufacturers make brief cases, so an entire chapter could be written on them. Just remember the brief case is one of the most visible business tools

## Chapter 10
### Dr. Travel Prescribes: Wheels of Fortune

that sends a message about how you do business. Hard cases may protect the contents, but they scream "I am conservative!" A leather case, especially soft-sided such as a lawyers brief or messenger bag with a lock, indicates you have important business dealings and you want the world to know it. It says you are serious about doing business. A canvas or nylon brief case shows you are more casual, but still professional.

I have several brief cases. In each instance they are an extension of my business personality. In business, men are categorized by their briefcase, watch, tie, pen, and shoes. Women are categorized by their briefcase or multipurpose bag, pen, daytimer, watch, shoes, nails, and hair. For both men and women, you never have a chance to make a second first impression.

I accessorize for the audience. I purchase products that fit my personality without offending the potential client or supplier. Casual clients require casual accessories. Think about how you react to someone whose tattered briefcase does not match their well tailored suit, pressed shirt, and designer tie.

**Doctor's Travel Bag(s).** A Mulholland Brothers messenger bag, which looks like a letter carrier's bag, provides lots of room, can collapse into luggage and expand. These qualities make this bag one of my favorites. Made of natural leather, the bag gets more golden in color with each time I used it. Mulholland makes some of the most unique and durable bags I have found anywhere in the world. For more information, call 888-744-3847 or look on the web at http;//www.jfainc.com.

Another is my lawyer's brief case from the London Harness Company, with accordion organizer partitions inside. The top handle allows the weight to balance in my hand, instead of pulling at my shoulder. The oversized flap covers the partitions. This brief case has two straps to keep it closed (in case it's overstuffed and cannot be locked closed). The leather in this briefcase is the same material used for English riding saddles — a hard leather that still feels like new. The leather is rigid but colors beautifully. Per directions

Part I:
Get Ready for Take-Off

from the retailer, I have scratched the leather with my fingernails and sprayed it with water to make it age more rapidly. I have no information about the manufacturer but it was purchased from Asburys of London, in the Trump Tower in New York. When I carry the bag, it says "Wow! This could have been his father's or grandfather's. Way cool!"

A third bag, made of rosewood, is from Luxurious Wood Accessories. Even writing about it sounds stuffy. It is a spectacular piece of furniture intended to be a visual message that I am important and don't need lots of paper, pens, or a laptop to do business. This wooden briefcase has no storage value except to carry one contract or a small file to a meeting. I only carry this briefcase to a meeting after I have completed the sale.

My fourth bag is a Coach Organizer Computer Case that enables me to carry my laptop without announcing to the world I am carrying a computer. Accordion partitions in the front enable me to open the case without revealing the laptop in the back partition. Without the laptop in place, the back section provides ample room for large files, magazines, work papers, and so forth.

Finally, I have my Hartmann hard-sided organizer briefcase. This brief case, given to me by my staff in 1979, has seen most of the world and looks like it. When I carry this case, I tell my audience I am traditional, conservative, and concerned with classic values. This case never gets compliments or criticism. Just a few ". . . you really have been all over the place, haven't you?"

Remember to choose your brief case as you choose your watch, shoes, tie, and other accessories.

***Carry-on, duffel, and roller bags.*** Name a price, style, color, material, or design and you'll discover a treasure chest of choices. For some reason travelers from the Orient like the hard-sided bags, while the U.S. traveler embraces the carry-on with wheels.

100

# Chapter 10
## Dr. Travel Prescribes: Wheels of Fortune

Carrying your own bag on a flight means you avoid waiting at the luggage carousel and you save on the wear and tear of your bag, but you are required to "lug n' age". If you are going to carry-on, do not carry on about your bag's weight, the lack of space on board the aircraft, complaints from other passengers trying to avoid being struck by your bags as you move through the cabin. Also remember current airline specifications for overhead luggage are 10"×14"×36" (reduced to 28" on some carriers) and under the seat requirements are 9"×14"×22." If you can lift the piece of luggage, there is currently no weight restriction, but that may change in the near future.

I have seen many passengers try to stuff air conditioners, big screen televisions, and Mexican sundials into the overhead compartments of domestic airlines. On a recent United flight the overhead compartment had a special mesh screen that had to be removed before you could gain access to the luggage. The screen was revealed after the compartment door was opened. So it became a two-step process to prevent the luggage, which may have shifted during the flight, from falling on a seated passenger. Neat idea.

1) Are you sure you want to carry on your luggage? If the answer is yes, what do you need on board?

2) *Hard- or soft-sided luggage?* Hard-sided luggage provides the best protection, but it is not forgiving when pushed into an over head compartment. It simply won't give. It takes up the same amount of space empty or full and it provides the greatest wrinkle-free packing. Hard-sided cases break before they bend. Make sure the wheels, locks, and frames can take the abuse. I like Halliburton (aluminum) and Pelican products (molded plastic). Both companies make camera bags with foam inserts. The bags have an *O* ring seal so water and dirt cannot get into the bags. Because they are hard, a good lock keeps private all your privates. Soft luggage can survive more abuse, overstuffing, and infrequent cleanings. Hard-sided luggage shows dents and scratches. Soft-sided does poorly with sharp objects. Zippers and seams give way under stress, so inspect the hardware and stitching. Make sure the handle is

Part I:
Get Ready for Take-Off

comfortable and attached well. Look at the straps . . . are they padded? Is the hardware durable and easy to use?

3) *Duffel, overnight or wheelies.* In nearly every instance these three types of bags are designed to give you access during the flight. Most have outside pockets, open on the side with a zipper that goes around the bag, or have easy top openings that let you to keep the bag under the seat in front of you.

I have two favorite carry-ons. The first is my Holland Brothers safari bag. The second is my TravelPro Platinum RollAboard. I place the TravelPro in the overhead and the safari bag under the seat in front of me. I have full access to the safari bag and I can get into the TravelPro with little effort.

4) *Garment bags* are designed to hold a suit or dress. They fold in the middle. Again, they come in various designs, colors, materials, and with or without wheels. I prefer the Samsonite Two-Suiter. It is small and when folded in half, it stands on its own. Remember, you must be an adult to use a garment bag. In other words, your clothes must be long enough to require the length or why bother. Because most porters do not want you to check a garment bag, arrive early and request a garment bag box from the airline. You can obtain this box, at no charge, from the oversize or late check-in counter. Your bag can be opened to lay flat. Once you arrive at your destination, save the box, if possible, for the return trip. Make sure you put your name on the box, as well as on your luggage.

## Bags you take on vacation

*Suitcase.* Like every other piece of luggage I have discussed, suitcases come in every material imaginable. For instance, Mulholland Brothers offers an American Alligator 32" suitcase for $32,750 and Pierre Cardin offers a nested four- (4) piece set of luggage for $89. If you sailed on the Titanic, in First Class, you had a matched set of Pullmans. These hard-sided trunks, boxes, and accessory carriers contained features that kept the clothes wrinkle-free and organized. Rectangular boxes with hinged lids, Pullmans of yesterday are no

# Chapter 10
## Dr. Travel Prescribes: Wheels of Fortune

longer found on many domestic airline carousels or cruise cabins. The closest bag readily available and affordable is the vertical Pullman called an EZCart by American Touristor and its parent, Samsonite. It is a large, upright "wheelie" that is soft-sided and can be pushed or pulled. I use my EZCart for any trip in which I don't need to pack many business clothes. The large, open cavity offers three detachable shelves. The large zippered top has a waterproof section which holds a suit in the provided carrier.

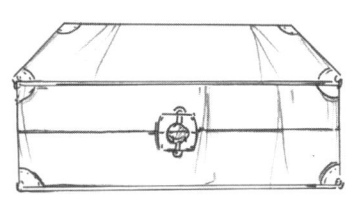

On trips to Hawaii, Aruba, or Puerto Rico or on a cruise, I pack shorts, T-shirts, underwear, sneakers, and sandals on each shelf. Once I arrive, I wheel my luggage next to the dresser drawer and unload in the same order I packed. I take one dark suit, a clean white shirt, braces (suspenders), and a tie. All of this is packed in a dry cleaner's plastic garment bag to avoid wrinkling. Normally, it comes back home in the same condition as it left . . . still unwrinkled, inside the cleaner's bag.

My other, larger garment bag is a Hartmann 54" Four-Suiter. It cannot be carried on the plane. I purchased the wheel kit so I could pull it through the airport, but have found I must balance the contents or it falls over. Because I have already packed when I discover the bag is out of balance I look for a porter or unfold my luggage cart. I chose the ladies (54") instead of the man's (48") because it has several extra inches that hold a man's raincoat without extra folding.

I recently purchased a TravelPro Platinum Fold-Over Garment Bag with wheels. While this is a nice bag, I would not recommend it for more than one suit. It folds over and zips closed making it difficult to pack more than one suit. This bag does have wheels but it does not fit into some of the overhead compartments on older aircraft. If you want a garment bag refer to the previous section. If you want to ship your clothes, get a bag that gives you enough room to hold more than two suits. I rarely travel with only one suit. If the meeting is important enough for a suit, I take two, in case of stains, rips, or surprise dinner engagements.

## Travel Kit/Cosmetic Pouch.

If diversities exist in luggage, this is the catagory that sets new standards. Every material available in the world and every claim of huge storage capabilities, come neatly packed in each kit. Before you purchase a travel kit, ask yourelf:

- ✓ Is it waterproof inside?
- ✓ Will it hold all your tolietry needs including your electric toothbrush, shampoo, conditioner, toothpaste, razor, dental floss, and cologne?
- ✓ Is the zipper or closing mechanism strong enough so you won't find the contents spilled all over your clothes?
- ✓ Have you chosen function over form or name brand? This kit/pouch will be used and abused.

Go to a discount store, or look for a free kit during promotional periods for women's and men's fragrance lines in major department stores. Spending money on leather or alligator is a waste of money. Leather adds weight you don't need and it won't stand up to shampoo and perfume spilling on its surface.

## Passport/Ticket Holder.

Most luggage companies also offer some form of passport cover or travel organizer. The best ones hold both your passport and airline or cruise tickets. If the outside is zippered, you are assured the contents will not fall out during travel. Coach offers the best travel organizer I have seen. While expensive, the zippers are strong, the organization is well done, and offers an outside zipped coin pocket, so you can place a phone call while

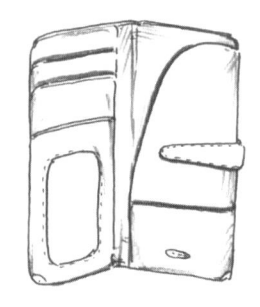

# Chapter 10
## Dr. Travel Prescribes: Wheels of Fortune

waiting for your luggage. Go into a Coach store and see one.

### ✈Travel Tip: Some More Packing Tips.

Place at least two luggage tags, with the same address, on the outside of each bag. Often the outside tag gets ripped off. Using two tags reduces this possibility. If the luggage is lost, the airline may try to open the luggage. Place a luggage tag inside your luggage. Tape it to the inside cover or somewhere easy to see. Do not put your home address on any luggage tag. Use your business address instead.

Take your medicine. Do not pack any items you may need within twenty-four hours. Never leave tickets, passports, visas, prescriptions, or other important materials inside your luggage. Also, remember the inside of the airline or cruise cabin may get very hot in the summer. Keep your cosmetics cool or you will find a lipstick popsicle that will make your blush run. Do not forget you can normally replace anything you forgot. Enjoy the trip and don't sweat the small stuff.

If you have been counting, you discovered I have at least five briefcases, two carry-ons, three suitcases, and lots of duffel bags, gym bags, and other pieces of luggage purchased or given to me over the years. I have found certain features that I like in each bag. Because I travel over 200 days a year, normal wear and tear force me to always be on the lookout for a new piece of luggage. As you read this section, drop me an email and tell me what you think is the best piece of luggage and why. Write to me at jfeldman@doctor-travel.com.

Part I:
Get Ready for Take-Off

You can find luggage in plenty of locations. Some of the manufacturers are listed below, with their U.S. toll free (800) or 888 numbers. You can also link to one of our suppliers which offers many types of luggage, http://www.jfainc.com to order.

| | | |
|---|---|---|
| American Tourister | ✈ | (800) 635-5505 |
| Andiamo Luggage | ✈ | (800) 433-8711 |
| Atlantic Luggage | ✈ | (888) ATLANTIC |
| Boyt Luggage | ✈ | (800) 366-2689 |
| Bugatti | ✈ | (800) 284-2887 |
| Coach | ✈ | (800) 223-8647 |
| Delsey | ✈ | (800) 558-3344 |
| Eagle Creek | ✈ | (619) 471-7600 |
| Eddie Bauer | ✈ | (800) 789-1386 |
| Ghurka | ✈ | (800) 243-4368 |
| Hartmann Luggage | ✈ | (800) 331- 0613 |
| Hermes | ✈ | (800) 441-4488 |
| Holland Brothers | ✈ | (888) 520-2435 |
| Lark | ✈ | (800) 421-LARK |
| Louis Vitton | ✈ | (800) 285-2255 |
| Patagonia | ✈ | (800) 638-6464 |
| Pelican Products | ✈ | (800) 473-5422 |
| Polo/Ralph Lauren | ✈ | (800) 653-7656 |
| Samsonite | ✈ | (800) 262-8282 |
| Sharper Image | ✈ | (800) 344-4444 |

TravelPro ✈ (800) 741-7471

Tumi Luggage ✈ (800) 322-8864

Zelco Industries ✈ (800) 431-2486

Zero Halliburton ✈ (801) 299-7355

Luggage & Leather Goods ✈ (800) 862-4224
Manufacturers of America
*(Provides general information*
*on airline regulations*
*and manufacturers)*

Part I:
Get Ready for Take-Off

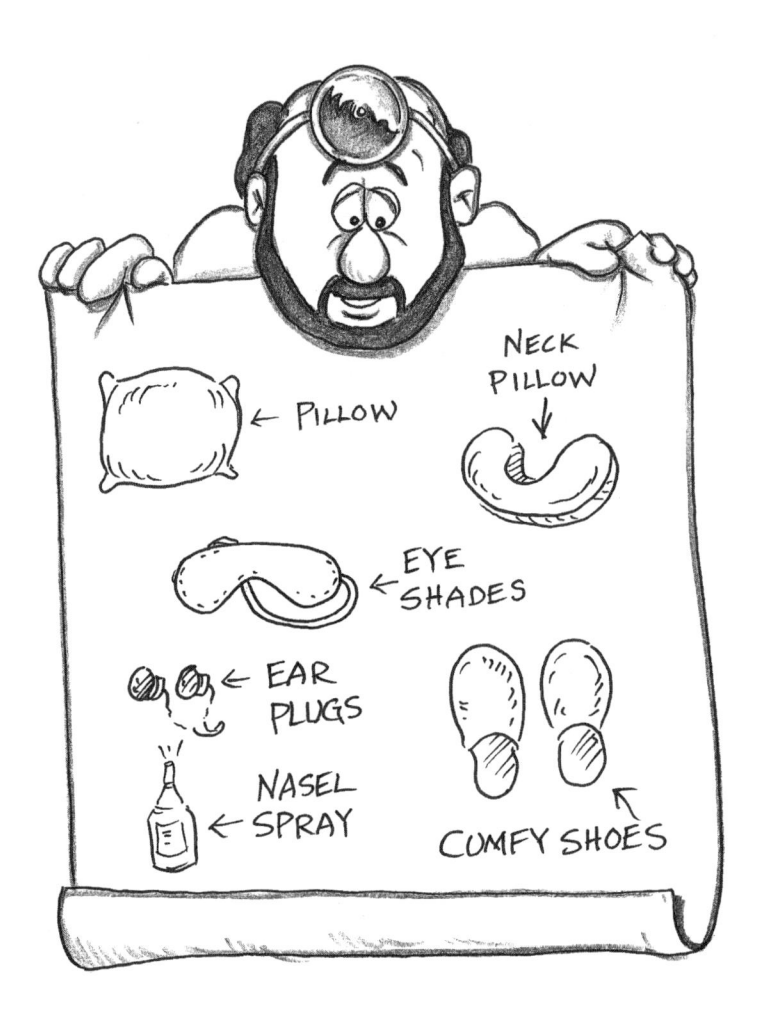

## Chapter 11
# Special Travel Needs

Air travel can be a hassle for anyone. But for the elderly, the disabled, or those traveling with small children, additional challenges occur. This chapter provides helpful hints on handling those special needs.

## Travel Secret: Suggestions for Seniors

Most of the information in this book (like ordering special meals, making duplicates of important papers, elevating your feet on your carry-on, and so forth) apply to older, as well as to other travelers. But a few recommendations apply especially to seniors.

- Ask for special senior fares or buy coupon books that give you a set amount of flights for a flat fee.

- Consider taking duplicates of items that would make your trip miserable if lost — like prescription glasses, dentures, medicines, and so forth.

- Dress in layers — it often gets chilly on the plane. Also, take along a pair of slipper-socks if you are going to take off your shoes.

- If you have difficulty walking in the airport terminal, order a wheelchair. There is no extra charge. If you forgot to request one for your destination, the pilot can radio ahead.

Part I:
Get Ready for Take-Off

## Travel Secret: Have Handicap, Will Travel

Because of the varied nature of disabilities, only a handful of suggestions for those with impaired mobility, hearing, or sight can be presented here.

- If you are physically challenged, seek a travel agent who understands your special requirements.
- In a wheelchair? If you request assistance in boarding the plane, you'll be the first to board, but probably the last to deplane. Give yourself extra time if you're changing planes. To play it safe, double the minimum flight connection time.
- When making plane reservations, request a bulkhead seat. It has more knee room.
- When making room reservations, make sure all facilities, such as bathrooms and public areas, are accessible. Also, ask for the lowest floor on which accessible services are available. In an emergency, rescue teams can get you out faster.
- When renting a car, ask for a two-door. It has extra room to move from the wheelchair to the car seat.
- If you are hearing or visually impaired, contact the hotel in advance to make sure they can accommodate your seeing-eye dog, have volume control telephones and visual devices to alert you if an alarm sounds, the phone rings, or someone knocks on the door.
- If you are visually impaired, when you reserve accommodations, ask if someone can give you a tour of the hotel/motel upon arrival. Also, ask if elevator signs and door numbers are in Braille. Once you're checked in, put a rubber band around the door knob to help you find the right door.

*We have a son now. We had a child so we can board the airlines earlier.*
–Dennis Miller

# Chapter 11
## Dr. Travel Prescribes: Special Travel Needs

> *Some people try to get their babies to sit down on flights, by giving them sedatives. On our doctor's suggestion, we tried this on a cross-country flight, and all it did was make Robert cranky. The only thing that cheered him up was to grab the hair of the man sitting in front of us, who tried to be nice about it, but if you have a nine-month-old child with a melted Hershey bar all over his pudgy little fingers grabbing your hair all the way from sea to shining sea, you'd start to get a little cranky yourself. So I think it might be a good idea if, on flights featuring babies, the airline distributed sedatives to all the adults, except the pilot.*
> — Dave Barry

## Travel Secret: Trekking with Tykes

- Travel during off-peak hours. Fewer passengers mean you have a better chance of an empty seat next to you.

- Take nonstop flights when possible because they take the least amount of time to get to your destination. Kids are less apt to get cranky and you don't have to change planes.

- Before your trip, read books about your destination to your kids. This helps them become interested in your trip.

- If your plane ride is a long one, schedule a night flight when kids are more apt to fall asleep.

- When you book your ticket, order a special children's meal. Also, take along extra snacks — hungry kids can't wait for meal service.

- Infants younger than two fly free on domestic flights. Ask about discounts for children two to eleven years old, or watch the newspaper ads for special "Kids Fly Free" deals.

- Airlines usually will not allow children under five to fly alone. For kids ages five to eleven, most airlines have escort programs. Some charge for this service, some don't; check with the carrier.

Part I:
Get Ready for Take-Off

> *What do you do to make your flight more fun? Talk to passengers and get them to tell jokes.*
> — Roblee, age 8,
> Saratoga Springs, FL

- Look for special children's playrooms at some airports.

- The best seat on the plane for kids? Consider window seats for short flights and aisles if they want to see the movie. Also, front row bulkheads may have more leg room, but they also lack under seat storage, have armrests that may not lift, and poor movie screen sight-lines. Rear rows are generally less crowded but noisier. Seats near the kitchen are usually also near the bathroom, but they are noisier and less private. Over-the-wing seats have poor window views.

- If you're a nursing mother, ask for a window seat, for more privacy.

- Most airlines don't provide safety seats for infants or toddlers. Consider taking along your own car seat if you're not going to hold the child on your lap. You must purchase a ticket if your child occupies a seat.

- On the plane, ask if kids can visit the cockpit before take-off.

- Take along entertainment — like storybook cassettes, puzzles, coloring books, card games, comics, stickers, and so forth. Small surprises packed in separate bags are better than giving kids everything at once.

- Infants need a pacifier to keep their ears clear. Older children can be given chewing gum.

- Some hotels have special children's programs and/or a babysitting service. Ask about these services.

I had a client who wanted to take her entire family to London in celebration of her second wedding. She planned to take all her immediate family and their significant others and children. She required all adults to fly in First Class. I suggested the children, six-eighteen years old, fly in coach. I called each child and asked the following: "What type of music do you listen to? CD or tape?" "What kind of video game system do you have? Nintendo, Sony, whatever." In each case, I asked for a few suggestions about titles they did not currently own.

In addition, I obtained several Sony Personal Video Walkmans. This allowed me to bring movies for each age group. I brought extra batteries — AA, AAA, 9 volt, and C — for all the players. Over twenty-five movies, fifty CDs and tapes, and dozens of video game cartriges kept the entire group occupied for the duration. They were so busy, in fact, many of the parents left their cozy First Class seats to check-in with the kids who did not care to be bothered. Even with the cost of all these extras I saved my client thousands of dollars by purchasing coach instead of First Class tickets for everyone.

If you join one of the membership lounges operated by most airlines, you can gain a great deal of assistance in your special travel needs. In many cases, a uniformed staff member will meet you at the ticket counter and escort you to the plane for early boarding or into the lounge while you wait for the flight. I suggest you evaluate the small cost versus the great benefits these clubs offer you.

> *I always get to the airport an hour early. That way, I can be one of the first to know the flight has been delayed.*
> — Robert Orben

# 2

# Off and Skipping

*Part II is entitled "Off and Skipping" instead of "Off and Running" because, if the reader is running, he or she is probably late, stressed out, and not enjoying the journey. The image of skipping, on the other hand, is more joyous, and a kinder, gentler way of traveling. It's hard to be somber and skip at the same time. Try it!*

*In the space age, man will be able to go around the
world in two hours —
one for flying and the other to get to the airport.*
— Neil H. McElroy,
former U.S. Secretary of Defense

# Chapter 12
# Get Me to the Airport on Time

## ✈Travel Tip: Beat the Clock... Not!

If you can't get to the airport, you aren't going anywhere. So always allow extra time to reach the airport. If it takes thirty minutes to get to the airport, don't allow thirty-one and still expect to be on time for your flight.

Remember, arriving at the airport an hour early and having to wait for your flight is far better than arriving an hour late and having to wait three hours for the next flight. Arriving early gives you time to check in, deal with lengthy lines, and negotiate the airport maze (especially if you are unfamiliar with some of the larger terminals).

If you have a boarding pass, it's fine to reach the gate fifteen minutes prior to departure — but play it safe: twenty minutes or more is much safer. If you don't have a boarding pass, make sure you check in at least thirty minutes before your flight is scheduled to leave. Your seat can be reassigned to someone else if you do not

Part II
Off and Skipping

## Travel Tip: Before You Go

✓ Check your tickets as soon as you get them. Make sure your tickets have the correct destination, date, and time of your flight. (One time my travel agent mistakenly sent me someone else's tickets. If I hadn't examined them, I would have been in Boise when I should have been in Birmingham!)

✓ Verify from which airport your flight will depart. Major cities frequently have several airports. I recall offering to drive some friends to catch their flight. Half-way to the San Francisco International Airport, they informed me they were leaving from Oakland.

✓ Use the phone. Call the airlines before you leave for the airport to see if your flight has been delayed or canceled. If it has, switch to plan B (which you should have considered when you booked your flight).

✓ Keep abreast of local weather and traffic conditions. Rain and road repair can substantially increase your travel time to the airport.

> *If the Lord had wanted people to fly, He would have made it simpler to get to the airport.*
> — Milton Berle

## Car, Cab, or Coach?

Other than walking, three kinds of transportation exist that you can take to any major airport. Each means of transportation has its pros and cons:

- **Private Transportation:**
*Your car*

+ Convenient
+ No waiting to be picked up

- Inconvenient if a traffic jam occurs
- Prohibitive parking expense for long trips
- Parking lots full during certain times of year

*Rental car*

+ Convenient
+ No waiting to be picked up
- Inconvenient if you don't know the route or if there is traffic
- You may have to return the car prior to taking the flight

*Taxi*

+ Convenient
- Expensive

> *Have you noticed every year it costs less to fly to Europe and more to get to the airport?*
> — Joey Adams

- **Semiprivate Transportation:**

*Shared Van or Shuttle Service (where available)*

+ Same convenience of a taxi (door-to-door service)
+ Less expensive than a taxi
- Makes multiple (but limited) stops

- **Public Transportation:**

*Bus or Train*

+ Less expensive than a taxi or van service
+ Rail service often beats rush hour traffic
- No door-to-door service
- Need to adhere to their schedule
- Frequent stops

Whatever means of transportation you take to get to the airport, leave extra time to get there and have a contingency plan should things go awry. If a traffic jam occurs, can you take a different route? If your van or shuttle doesn't show, can you take your own car, call a cab, or ask a friend or co-worker to take you?

> *Air travel will be much safer when they eliminate the automobile ride between the city and the airport.*
> — Anonymous

## ✈Travel Tip: Consider the Options

- When you're trying to decide between taking a cab or a shuttle, ask yourself "How many people are traveling?" If you're the only one, the shuttle is more cost-effective. Make sure you know in advance how many stops the shuttle will make, though. If the shuttle makes frequent stops, opt, instead, for a cab.

- Weigh your time and cost in taking a bus, train, or shared van service as opposed to taking a taxi. Sometimes the extra work or rest time gained by taking a cab far exceeds the cost.

## ✈Travel Tip: Make It a Repeat Performance

If you travel often and take your car to the airport, park it in the same place each time. Parking in the same place makes locating your car easier when you return.

I am often reminded of a personal experience that led me to live Murphy's Law firsthand. I had met a woman I wanted to introduce to my parents. I reasoned, if I flew to Florida, where my parents were on vacation, they would be in a great mood — relaxed and unable to find flaws in my new relationship. At the time, my mother was intent that I only date and, of course, eventually marry, someone Jewish.

I was nervous about the flight and the meeting. I packed and repacked, shampooed, shaved, and showered. I even doused myself in expensive aftershave.

# Chapter 12
## Dr. Travel Prescribes: Get Me to the Airport on Time

I picked up my date with over two hours to get to the airport. Because the normal drive time was only thirty minutes, I knew I could "skip" through the airport. When I arrived at the airport, fifty minutes after leaving my home, no skycaps were available. Because we needed to park the car, I suggested my date take the car and I would deal with the tickets and luggage.

I stopped the car and tried to open the trunk, only to find I did not have the trunk key. Apparently, I had separated the trunk key from the ignition key when I valet-parked the car a day earlier. So here we were, trying to decide what to do at O'Hare Airport, when one of Chicago's finest came by and told me to unload the trunk and move on. Because I could not open the truck, I told him about the problem. The police officer radioed a tow truck. Sensing his intention was to tow the car, I began to argue. Unknowingly, the officer was calling the tow truck to help open the trunk. He wrote me a ticket for parking in a no parking zone.

I was still determined to get to Florida. I reasoned we could purchase whatever we needed upon arrival. We parked the car and walked back to the terminal. Only then did I realize the airline tickets were in the outside pocket of the suitcase, packed in the car trunk. I had run out of time, patience, and the ability to rationalize "all would be well." At this point, I called it quits.

These situations are not unusual. Make sure you have your tickets and enough time for delays. Prepare for Murphy to take the trip with you. You never know when he will want to come along for the ride.

Part II
Off and Skipping

*Those were the days — it almost hurts to think about them — when Idlewild itself was a sight-seeing destination, when a trip to the airport, just to eat at the restaurant, or walk around the fountain, or go up in the control tower (they allowed you to do that then), promised glamour, excitement, and the awe of travel.*
— James Kaplan

## Chapter 13
# All Airports Are Not Created Equal

With the current hub-and-spoke system, you frequently must change planes to get from your departure city to your destination. A big difference can occur, depending on where you do this, both in terms of your comfort and in making your connection. Some airports are better located, have better layouts, and provide more amenities than others.

You may, for example, have a statistically better chance of making a connection in Dallas than you would in Chicago or Denver in the middle of winter. In addition, certain airports have nicer features than others. While you may not go out of your way to land at these airports for these features, it's always nice to know what they offer if you unexpectedly wind up there.

Of course you can always pass the time at any airport by sitting and waiting for your plane, but many terminals have more to do than this. Here are some choices:

### ✈Travel Tip: Amuse Yourself

Several airports have environments that come very close to amusement parks. My personal favorite is the underground mov-

Part II
Off and Skipping

ing sidewalk that connects United's B and C terminals in Chicago's O'Hare Airport. As you glide along, you are surrounded by a mirrored ceiling with changing neon lights, curved rainbow-colored walls on both sides, and new age music to soothe you.

## ✈Travel Tip: Catch Up on Culture

Although many passengers don't realize it, airports are filled with high-quality works of art. They contain collections by both local and international artists comparable to some museums. In addition, an airport's budget for artwork often rivals those of museums. Denver's new airport, for example, has $6.5 million set aside for art purchases.

With this much money being spent on art, it would be a waste if you did not stop for at least a moment and enjoy it or linger a bit longer when you have more time. Also, unlike museums with limited hours, airport art can be viewed twenty-four hours a day. Here are some airports where you can feast your eyes:

*John F. Kennedy International (International Arrivals Building):* More than 200 works of art including Miro, Calder, and Picasso.

*Seattle-Tacoma International (Concourse B):* An interactive sound-and-light art piece where passengers can change the wall-sized patterns by pressing four computer buttons.

*Boston Logan International (Terminal C):* Contains several unusual sculptures. One has angled nine-inch square mirrors that reflect passersby in a fun-house effect. Another plays bits of music.

*Miami International:* Amuse yourself with a series of constantly changing TV monitors including some that spell MIAMI.

*Orlando International:* Art can assist you in finding your car. Each floor of the garage contains sculptures of different creatures, such as alligators, flamingos, and wild pigs. The artwork helps you remember if you left your car on the "armadillo level" or the "frog floor."

# Chapter 13
## Dr. Travel Prescribes: All Airports Are Not Created Equal

*San Francisco's International* (United domestic terminal) has frequently changing exhibits, featuring such whimsical displays as taxis, birdhouses, sculptures, surf boards, or carousel horses.

> *If you have to travel by air and connect at a hub, carry a bandage with you and wrap it around your ankle. They will call an electric cart for you.*
> — Charles Kuralt

## ✈Travel Tip: Invest Your Time

At Pittsburgh International, you can get free stock quotes, as well as business news on computer terminals provided by a bank. San Francisco International, United terminal, has phone lines that will connect you with the Internet or your e-mail.

## ✈Travel Tip: Keeping Kids Content

Seattle-Tacoma airport has a Kids' Playport with scale-model planes for climbing, a simulated cockpit, a refueling truck, and a control tower that looks out on real runways. Pittsburgh International and Raleigh-Durham Airports have similar environments to keep kids entertained. A number of other airports around the country have specifically designed play areas run by children's museums in those cities.

Older kids can also entertain themselves at video arcades found at nearly every airport.

## ✈Travel Tip: Looking Good

Most major airports have shoeshine stands and both beauty and barbershops. If you have a few hours to spare, you can spruce up. Some of the latter (Great Cuts barbershop at San Francisco International and Hairlines salon at Seattle-Tacoma International) even have showers.

You can also find shower facilities at Honolulu International (minihotel, central lobby) and Miami International (airport hotel health club). For fifty cents, use the public showers in the rest rooms at Kansas City International and Phoenix Sky Harbor.

## ✈Travel Tip: Pray Away the Flight Delay

A number of airports (including Chicago's O'Hare International and New York City's Kennedy International) have chapels of various denominations and Miami's International (between concourse C and D) has a meditation room. These are tranquil places to get away from airline hustle and bustle or to pray your flight will leave on time.

## ✈Travel Tip: Read All About It

Milwaukee's General Mitchell International's main departure floor has a large secondhand bookstore where you can inexpensively browse away your wait.

> *When you travel by plane, wear a hat with a light on it because unaccompanied miners get on first.*
> — Ken Braly

## ✈Travel Tip: Shop 'Til You Drop

If you must shop, do it in style. New York City's Kennedy International has a Bloomie's Express (a boutique version of the upscale Bloomingdale's department store) on the third floor of the arrivals building.

Bring back some local color by shopping at the minimall of shops associated with the Pacific Northwest at Oregon's Portland airport. Or, take a short shuttle to Mall of America when you have a stopover in Minneapolis. Shopaholics can wander through the seventy-six stores in the retail mall at Pittsburgh International.

Two kinds of running exist: The kind athlete's do and running in the real world, which entails trying to get somewhere on time. Real-world running needs its own championships and recognized events. I suggest the following:

# Chapter 13
## Dr. Travel Prescribes: All Airports Are Not Created Equal

### ✈Travel Tip: Smell the Flowers

Honolulu International Airport (lower level, main terminal) has lovely Japanese, Chinese and Hawaiian gardens, complete with fish swimming in the ponds.

### ✈Travel Tip: Win Some, Lose Some

McCarran International in Las Vegas has over 700 slot machines and electronic poker games throughout the terminal, including the baggage area. If you really win big, you can always dump your clothes and replace them with money. Remember, though, the airport slots have the lowest winner payoff settings in Vegas. If you must play, make it for your entertainment money only.

### ✈Travel Tip: Work It Out

Stuck in Phoenix due to bad weather? For a small fee, you can get a workout at the fitness center in terminal 3.

Many other airports, (like Miami and O'Hare International) have hotels, either right within their facilities or nearby, with gyms. Ask about using their health club for a few hours.

If you are on a tight budget, but still want to get a workout, try walking around the terminal. Pittsburgh's International main concourse, for example, is as long as two football fields laid end-to-end.

### ✈Travel Tip: Getting Your Zs

Minneapolis-St. Paul International now houses apartment-like rooms called *Ziosks*. For a small fee, you can use such amenities as a color TV, sofa, desk, and a clock radio with an alarm. They are perfect for a short nap on a long layover. Some also come with a bathroom and shower. Other airports (like Honolulu or Los Angeles International) have on-site minihotels that rent by the hour.

*Never Say 'Hi, Jack!' in an Airport*
— Book title by Terry
and Rocky Denton

Part II
Off and Skipping

## ✈Travel Tip: Hey, Look Me Over!

Airports are confusing places, especially if you have never been in a particular one before. In addition to the overwhelming size of some airports, which make gate connections mammoth treks, changes in flight numbers, departure times, and gates also add to the confusion. The best insurance against airport fowl-ups is to check and double check all aspects of your flight. All the airlines' in-flight magazines have diagrams of the major airports they use frequently. Keep a copy in your briefcase for future trips.

- Check and recheck the departure board before heading for your flight.
- Examine your ticket immediately after checking in for each leg of your journey. Sometimes agents accidentally take two flight coupons instead of one.
- Check your ticket for your mileage number. It should be on your ticket stub. If your mileage number is there, getting mileage credit for your flight will be easier. If it isn't there, make sure it's recorded when you check in.
- Check your mileage number again if you change carriers. Sometimes, because different airlines use different computers, the first airline will have it recorded but the second airline will not (even if it's printed on the ticket).

## ✈Travel Tip: Far from the Madding Crowd

The only relatively quiet places at crowded airports, other than chapels, are the airline executive clubs. No, you needn't be an executive to use them and you also needn't be a million-mile flier. All you must do is pay for the yearly membership cost each airline charges ($100 and up, plus a one-time application fee).

For this fee, you get complimentary coffee or tea, snacks, phones (usually free local calls), fax and copy machines, meeting rooms, and more — like shorter or no check-in lines. And quiet. No

# Chapter 13
## Dr. Travel Prescribes: All Airports Are Not Created Equal

incessant boarding and paging announcements can be heard here. But you will hear an army of business folks making phone calls. Still, the airline clubs are much quieter than the hustle and bustle of the terminal.

Is the steep annual fee worth it? If you're an occasional traveler, the answer probably is no. If you're a regular traveler, the answer probably is yes. Not necessarily for the free coffee or tea, the relative quiet, or line-less counters, but for that time when the entire East Coast is closed due to a blizzard and you're stranded for six hours. For those times, you'll be glad you joined . . . at least until they close at 10 P.M. and your flight isn't until 11:45 P.M.

If you don't belong to one of these elite clubs, you can still locate a quiet place at an airport. The best source for a peaceful getaway is at a gate just after the plane has taken off. The gate has emptied out of those people meeting arriving passengers and those waiting to board. Of course, as soon as that gate has another scheduled flight, you'll have to move to another "just-departed" location.

> *You can be sitting in Chicago, waiting for a flight to Boston, and you are told the aircraft you are supposed to take hasn't reached Dallas, much less Chicago, because it is raining in Phoenix.*
> — Cornish Hitchcock

## ✈Travel Tip: Familiarity Breeds Comfort

Each airport has its own personality and layout. Smart travelers try to stick with one carrier. Not only will your frequent flier awards accrue more quickly, but you also will get to know that specific carrier's procedures and gate locations. And when you have a close connection, knowing the shortest route from terminal A to terminal B can make the difference between making a flight and missing one. Short cuts and time savers exist. Don't be afraid to ask. If you're a member of the airline executive clubs, they will provide all the "insider" information you need.

Part II
Off and Skipping

If you aren't a member, try to find the special services representative from your airline. In Chicago, the most famous agent was Ginny Boroski from American Airlines. When Ginny retired, American named one of the terminal hallways Ginny Boroski Way. Her retirement party was attended by some of the most frequent flyers in the city of Chicago. Ginny's retirement has left a huge void in exemplary customer service at the Chicago Terminal for American Airlines. I really miss Ginny!

> *The Airport Half-Mile: A race to the gate, commencing with the last call for the flight. Contestants carry two suitcases, and the course must include one moving walkway, which is not moving, and 150 tourists coming the other way.*
> — Miles Kingston

*"Why is there mistletoe hanging over the baggage counter?"
asked the airline passenger, amid the holiday rush. The clerk
replied, "It's so you can kiss your luggage good-bye."*
— Seymour Rosenberg

# Chapter 14
# To Check...
# or Not to Check...
# That Is the Question

*S*chlep is a wonderfully picturesque Yiddish word that describes the process of carrying things around. But schlep means much more than simply transporting something from one place to another. This descriptive word also implies you lug, haul, drag, carry things with difficulty, and move laboriously. Schlep is an accurate description of what many people do at airports. And I used to be one of them. My three rules for checking luggage were:

Rule # 1: Never check

Rule # 2: Never check

Rule # 3: Never check

My rule changed, though, after I had to run from Gate #2A to Gate #376Z (well, almost) to make a close connection while carrying what seemed like 100 pounds of baggage. A few weeks later, my never-check policy was reexamined after I began to get severe neck

Part II
Off and Skipping

and back pains. Now I check my suitcase containing my clothing and I hand carry my irreplaceable things, such as my laptop, office work, and overnight necessities.

Checking luggage is a personal decision. If you don't mind lifting and lugging, then don't check your bags. But do be aware carrying your luggage on board may not be the best thing for your personal well-being. In addition to jet lag, you may also experience jet lug.

On the other hand, if you are willing to wait at the luggage carousel, then check your bags. Of course, the anxiety of waiting for a bag that doesn't show up may not be too good for your health either.

## ✈Travel Tip: On a Long Journey Even a Straw Weighs Heavy

You may want to keep this Spanish proverb in mind as you consider the reasons for checking versus carrying on your luggage.

**To Check –**
*The Advantages:*
- You don't have to schlep your stuff around.
- If the flight is delayed, you have far more freedom to move about the airport or travel into town.
- Because you have no need to store your bags, you can avoid the mad dash to board and find a bin.
- You needn't cram or lift your luggage into those spacious overhead bins.

**To Check –**
*The Disadvantages:*
- Your luggage may get lost or stolen.
- Your luggage may be opened and the contents may be removed.

*The scientific theory I like best is that the rings of Saturn are composed entirely of lost airline luggage.*
— Mark Russell

### . . . or Not to Check –
*The Advantages:*
- You can go right to the gate.
- You needn't wait in line at the ticket counter.
- You needn't wait at the luggage carousel.
- Your luggage wouldn't get misrouted or robbed.

*The Disadvantages:*
- You must schlep.

## ✈Travel Tip: Never Check

- Any medications.

- Any irreplaceable items (like the only copy of the soon-to-be-best-selling manuscript you just wrote).

- Valuable items, such as keys, jewelry, traveler's checks, or cash.

- Expensive luggage (this is a clue to thieves something of value maybe inside).

- Essentials. For example, Marjorie Yasueda, a senior travel consultant, who does a lot of mountain trekking, always carries her hiking boots aboard on the outbound leg of her journey. "There is no way I can break in new hiking boots when I'm in the Himalayas. Coming back, on the other hand, I check them," Yasueda says.

- Fragile or breakable items.

- Perishables. Planes get delayed and perishables spoil.

- A cigarette lighter or matches. You can't check them, but you can carry them aboard the plane in your pocket.

- Flammables, corrosives, and explosives.

- Firearms. Loaded firearms are forbidden. (Unloaded are allowed in checked bags if sealed, declared and labeled properly (the same applies to ammunition).

Part II
Off and Skipping

- Oral/rectal thermometers. If broken, the mercury could damage the planes structure and wiring.

> *Never check anything — ever — under any circumstances. Better to throw the bags away.*
> — Jay Leno

## ✈Travel Tip: If You Check:

- Remember all airlines limit the number (two or three), weight (seventy pounds), and size of your checked luggage. Excess fees are charged for over-the-limit, overweight baggage or oversized items. (Bicycles and surfboards have an excess charge, skies and golf clubs don't . . . go figure!)

- Consider the curbside check-in for less carrying and shorter lines. (If you want to see your bags on the other end of your trip, tip the handlers.) If you ask the handler to put on a First Class bag tag, your luggage will be loaded last and delivered first. I always tell the skycap I plan to upgrade at the ticket counter as I give him a $5 dollar bill. I wait to see that the First Class tag is placed on the bag and the bag is put on the conveyor belt. If I have more than one bag, I add $2 to the tip per bag.

- Check-in at least thirty minutes before flight time, but not more than ninety minutes (for domestic travel). Check a bag too early, and it may get overlooked.

- Remove all tags from previous trips to avoid confusing baggage handlers. I suggest removing the tags as soon as you get to your destination or once you return home.

A friend who travels all over the world keeps all his baggage tags on his luggage as if he were collecting ribbons at the county fair. On a trip to South Africa, he left his bag on the airplane. It took several months for its return. It seems the bag made a trip around the world . . . without him.

## Chapter 14
### Dr. Travel Prescribes: To Check ... or Not to Check ... That is the Question

- Examine the new tag being placed on your luggage. If it doesn't have the three-letter code of your destination, your bag is not going where you're going. PDX (Portland, Oregon) looks similar to PHX (Phoenix, Arizona) but, as you know, they are nowhere near each other. If you don't have the various destination codes, ask the airline for the specific code when you book your flight.

- Make sure you receive a baggage claim check for each piece of luggage checked. Count the claim checks in front of the handler.

- Your airline ticket may limit or exclude liability for the loss of such items as cameras, cash, or jewelry. If you are traveling with valuables, carry them with you. Prior to your trip, call your insurance agent to make sure what you plan to take on the trip is covered by at least one of your existing insurance policies.

- If your bag does not show up on the luggage carousel, make sure you fill out a claim form before you leave the airport and get a receipt!

- Consider purchasing excess valuation insurance if you feel the airline limit for lost luggage won't cover your contents.

> *I checked my luggage last week. The guy tore off the stubs and said, "Here are your lottery tickets."*
> — Gene Perret

- When making a connection, stick with the same airline. It minimizes foul-ups. The safest-to-least-safest ranking for avoiding lost luggage are:
    - ✓ Nonstop flights.
    - ✓ Through or direct flight (one or more stops but no change of plane).
    - ✓ Same line connection (change of plane but no change of carrier).
    - ✓ Interline connection (change of plane and carrier).

- If you are renting a car at your destination, save time by getting the rental paperwork done while the baggage is being processed.

- Think a second time about checking your bags at Kennedy, LaGuardia, Newark, Boston, Miami, or Los Angeles. According to the *Wall Street Journal*, these are the six worst airports in the U.S. for stolen luggage.

- Use luggage straps and locks for safe keeping.

- If traveling with someone else, each person can pack some clothes in the other's luggage to lessen the impact if one bag is lost or detained.

## ✈Travel Tip: Ninety-eight Percent of All Lost Bags Are Returned

Despite all the bad news about lost luggage, the good news is most luggage is not lost . . . it's only delayed (the airlines call it *misrouted*). Most of the time, this means your bags have simply visited a different city (sorry, no extra frequent flier miles for the detour). Less frequently, this may mean your luggage has been stolen or *permanently misrouted*.

The other good news about misrouted luggage is, with the advent of zebra-striped bar codes and sophisticated scanning devices, bags that have gone astray are often quickly located and redirected to you within hours.

## ✈Travel Tip: If Your Bags Go Astray

- The last carrier is responsible for it — even if the first carrier goofed.

- Ask for cash for emergency purchases. If the baggage supervisor refuses, save all receipts and try to get a refund later.

- Claim any loss or damage within twenty-four hours (preferably before you leave the terminal). Get the agent's name and phone number in case the problem is not resolved to your satisfaction. And make certain the airline will deliver your bags without a charge when they are found. If you checked in on time, the airline will deliver them free.

> *As my father always says, 'There are two kinds of luggage — carry-on and lost.'*
> — Lilly Walters

- Keep your baggage claim tag or a photocopy. Your claim tag is proof your bag was checked.

- Currently, the limit you can claim for lost luggage is $1,250. The value of lost items are figured at depreciated, rather than at replacement cost. And the amount is not per bag, but $1,250 total, which may soon increase.

- If your loss is more than $1,250, your household insurance policy may cover part of it.

## ✈ Travel Tip: If You Carry on

- Make certain your laptop computer is fully charged. You may be asked to turn it on by the security inspectors.

- Remember, in addition to your checked luggage, most airlines only allow two carry-ons, which must fit under the seat in front of you or in the overhead bins. Items not usually counted as carry-ons include overcoats, cameras, umbrellas, reading materials, and purses of a reasonable size.

- Under-the-seat carry-ons must be no more than 45" overall (length, height, and depth combined).

- Remember, too, luggage space differs on different planes: Airbus A320 and Boeing 737-300 have more room; McDonnell Douglas DC-10 and Boeing 757 have less.

- Avoid the bulkhead; it doesn't have under-seat storage.

- Consider boarding the plane as soon as you can to claim the overhead bin space.
- Try not to place your bag in an overhead bin behind you or you'll have to buck the tide when the plane unloads.
- Never, ever leave your bags unattended.
- Don't carry your bags over one shoulder. Balance the distribution of weight to ease neck and back strain.

The choice of checking or carrying baggage continues to be monitored by the airlines. Recently, several airlines issued statements saying they were going to reduce the number and size of carry-ons. Airlines have already stopped the use of luggage carts by demanding they fit beneath the seat in front of you. If you purchase a heavy-duty cart, and not one of those silly carts sold at most airports, it will be difficult to make it fit under the seat. The roll-aboard luggage provides the best of both situations. These bags come in various shapes and sizes, have long handles that enable you to pull them behind you, and now some offer locking handles that enable you to push them. Make sure the roll-aboard is accepted by the airlines for overhead or beneath-the-seat storage in advance of your flight.

> *Among the items passengers have insisted on carrying on are a small robot, the drive shaft from a BMW, a four-foot fig tree, a five-foot lamp with a four-foot shade, a 500-pound computer, and a ten-foot assembly of tree limbs, grass, and leaves with a bird's nest in the middle.*
> — Jean Heller

*Having a wonderful time. Wish I was here.*
— bumper sticker

# Chapter 15
# The Zen of Flying

When you travel by air, you have little or no power over such things as weather delays, mechanical failures, or screaming babies. But even though the situation may be out of your control, you can use your inner resources to turn those Maalox moments into more manageable ones.

We all have the capacity to control our feelings so we don't let uncontrollable situations ruin our day. Here are some suggestions:

## ✈Travel Tip: Be Here Now

In the Zen tradition, the emphasis is on being present in the moment. This concept revolves around the idea that if you are worried about the past or if you are apprehensive about the future, this does not allow you to be aware of — let alone enjoy — what you are experiencing right now.

For example, if a late departure occurs and you constantly worry about the possibilily of missing your connection, not only will you miss enjoying the first leg of the trip, even if something wonderful did happen, you probably wouldn't notice it. Try to concentrate on what is happening in this moment and no other.

## ✈Travel Tip: Take a Deep Breath

When we get upset, we get tense. When we're tense, we tend to take short, shallow breaths, which only adds to our stress. Quiet your mental chatter, take control, and reduce your stress with some deep, slow breathing.

This not only works wonders for travel aggravations, but also for tackling turbulence. For me, turbulence is a reminder to meditate, to watch my breath. Like the Zen master's bell, it tells me to stop whatever I'm doing and focus on my breathing. Watching my breath calms me until the bumpiness has passed.

Try inhaling and exhaling to a set count. For example, slowly count to eight while inhaling and then do the same when exhaling:

L-o-n-g, s-l-o-w, d-e-e-p breaths.

Again, l-o-n-g, s-l-o-w, d-e-e-p breaths.

L-o-n-g, s-l-o-w, d-e-e-p breaths.

Repeat until you're calm.

An article in the *National Business Employment Weekly* about relieving stress noted: "Deep breathing clears your mind, refocuses your energy, cleanses your lungs, and increases your body's oxygen supply." "The technique," says the author of the article, Myra Ellen Edelstein, "is so simple that people often forget to use it."

> *A journey of 1,000 miles begins with a single delay of two hours before takeoff.*
> — Bob Levey

# Chapter 15
## Dr. Travel Prescribes: The Zen of Flying

## ✈Travel Tip: Create Your Own Airport Ritual

- *As long as they don't answer back –*

Rita Derbas, an innovation consultant (who doesn't mind the middle seat), talks to her suitcases and tells them to go where she is going. "The check-in person laughs," she says, "but so far I've not had any luggage lost or delayed that I've talked to."

- *Soul food –*

Melinda Henning, founder of Doing Business By Phone™ has a preboarding calm-down ritual. She always allows enough time to enjoy a cup of nonfat frozen yogurt, which she eats very slowly before boarding.

- *Repeat after me –*

Padi Selwyn, a professional speaker and author, uses a mantra to calm herself when flights are canceled or delayed. She repeats over and over again, "Well, everybody has to be somewhere. I guess this is where I have to be right now!"

For me, air travel is my chance to catch up on the numerous magazines, newsletters, and public relations notices I receive. I take highlighters, file folders, and a plastic kitchen trash bag. I start in the back of the book and look at the resource ads or last-page editorial. I move to the front and find the index. I scan the contents to see if an article or column I want to read is in the issue. If so, I highlight the title. Then I go to the last article I marked, back to front. I return to the front so I can focus on the ads and graphics, instead of the headlines that draw me into an article that "kills time." If an article has some merit, I tear it out of the magazine and put it into one of the folders. My folders are marked:

- Personal
- Resource Information
- Current Speaking
- Merchandise
- Travel Ideas

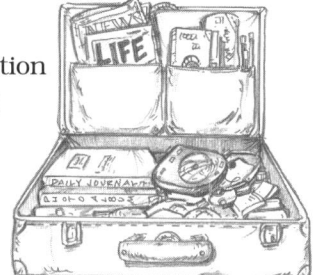

Part II
Off and Skipping

Once I finish the magazine, I place it in the plastic bag. This makes it easy either to recycle or retrieve. The process is part of the entire journey. I can read, write, and educate myself on topics I may not normally have the time or inclination to pursue.

### ✈Travel Tip: Remember It's a Process

Often we get so caught up in wanting to get to our destination, we forget about the journey itself. Getting from one place to another involves a process. Part of the process may be enjoyable and part may not. Focus on the former; forget the latter.

> *Nothing erases unpleasant thoughts more effectively than concentration on pleasant ones.*
> — Hans Selye

> *If we see ourselves as victims of circumstance or as victims of irrational forces beyond our control, the chances are that our distress will be intensified.*
> — Dr. Allen Fay

### ✈Travel Tip: When One Door Closes, Another Opens

One of my teachers left me with some unforgettable words. He said, "To want what you don't have is to waste what you do have."

If you are miserable about air travel, you are focusing on what you don't have instead of looking for what you do have. The next time you are delayed, relieve your stress by looking for what opportunity the delay has opened up for you.

For example, an executive I met from United Way told me he had been booked on three different flights with nine different reservations for a delay that totaled eighteen hours. He realized this long period of uninterrupted time gave him a chance to watch the U.S. Senate debates about the Persian Gulf War, something he would never have done if the delay hadn't occurred. Because of this, he said he had new confidence in the U.S. government and the democratic process.

In another instance, business consultant Rebecca Morgan turns annoying delays into productive scrap time by addressing her Christmas cards. Who cares if it's July? She's the first one on her block to have them finished.

I take birthday, anniversary, congratulations, and thank you cards with me when I travel. Sometimes I write a thank you card prior to the arrival at my destination. I may be visiting several hotels for consideration in our travel incentive programs. These hotels have taken the time to show me the property, perhaps invited me for a meal, or even to stay over night at no charge. A thank you goes a long way in firming up the relationship. Recently, I stayed at the Mandarin Oriental Hotel in Hawaii. We were unable to use the facilities due to the previous space commitments from other clients. I left thank you notes for all the staff who worked with me on the sight inspection, though. I received two phones calls from the hotel. In both cases, they were amazed I took the time to thank them and they offered me a complimentary return visit when I wanted to vacation in Hawaii. Both of the respondents informed me my thank note was much appreciated . . . and not the norm.

The doors of opportunity can be either physical things you can do around the airport or they can be directed inwardly as a wonderful time to work on your personal growth.

## ✈Travel Tip: Physical Opportunities

- When your flight is delayed, you now have some extra time. What wonderful thing can you do with this time?

- Tell yourself: "Someone or something is waiting for me at this airport." Your challenge is to discover what — or who — that wonderful something is.

Part II
Off and Skipping

- What book or magazine have you put off reading? Go to the airport bookstore. Buy and read it!
- Whose birthday or anniversary is coming soon? Go to the airport gift shop and find the perfect card for that person (you may even get the added bonus of a laugh or two while you select a card).

> *You know you can't avoid the idiots at airport security, the lines at ticket counters, people who are irritated, or the delays. You just have to develop a certain separate peace, to just go with the flow.*
> — David Brenner

- Phone home. One study found a simple call home to family or friends is an excellent stress buster.
- Ask yourself: Who's the person I've owed a letter for a long time? Then write a long letter.
- Misery loves company. Chat with your fellow passengers (it's easy to start a conversation with a delay or cancellation in common). Ask his or her funniest travel experience. Where do you think I found many of my stories? After you hear the story, ask him or her send it to me for possible inclusion in future books.

The other way to meet other passengers is to join one of the club lounges offered by the airlines and Diners Club. These facilities provide snacks, drinks, TV, comfortable settings, and a staff to assist you in making reservations at the local hotels, restaurants, or airlines. In most cases, the lounge is open early and remains open late. This privilege costs $125–$400, but a few delays, early arrivals, or meetings quickly make the investment worthwhile. I especially suggest these lounges to women who travel. They are a safer place to wait for a flight or to have a meeting.

- Play the "I-wonder-what-he-or-she-does?" game. Look around, choose someone, and imagine what he or she does.

Is he or she single or married? Have children? If so, how many? What kind of lifestyle does he or she live? The possibilities are endless!

*Inner growth opportunities —*

- Delayed flights give you a chance to test your patience. Ask yourself: How important will this delay seem five or ten years from now?
- Lost bags give you a chance to see how skillful you are at doing with less.
- When you don't get your meal right away, you are given a chance to examine your compassion for busy flight attendants.
- Crying children give you a chance to turn howls into music.
- When people push and shove or when there is overcrowding, you are given a chance to see how tolerant you can be.
- And, no matter what the circumstances, you are always given a chance to test your love for your fellow human beings.

One writer told me when things get really stressed, he gets up on a chair and yells, "Oh what an opportunity for growth and learning!" While this may not be the most appropriate action to take at airports, you can still look for those doors of opportunity.

> *Travel teaches you about traditions and tolerance; it teaches you about history and continuity; it teaches you about artistic creation and aesthetic ambition; it teaches you about the myriad differences that enrich the global mosaic, and about the importance of each and every piece in that mosaic. And, ultimately, travel teaches you about boundaries and boundlessness, and about the stresses and depths, the diminishings and enchantments of love.*
> — Donald W. George, travel editor,
> San Francisco *Chronicle*

Part II
Off and Skipping

During a chance meeting, I asked what my associate did for a living. He informed me he had just quit his job of twenty-one years as an IRS agent. Now he was faced with a career decision. What would he do with the rest of his life?

I suggested he form a counseling company for anyone with a problem with the IRS. I also suggested he come up with stories and suggestions about dealing with the IRS. After all, he had many years of experience upon which to rely. To convince him, I said everyone in the country was a possible attendee at a seminar or keynote speech. But he was still unsure about my suggestion.

I called the waitress over and asked her: "Would you be interested in attending a seminar that taught you how to deal with the IRS?" "Would I?" was her resounding response. "I owe the IRS over $500,000!"

"How can that be?" my associate asked. "Do you remember the big scandal with Michael Millikan years ago?" she asked. "Well, ten years after his trial, the IRS came to my house and told my husband they disallowed certain deductions, which resulted in an assessment of almost $1.5 million against us."

My associate turned to me and said, "You have changed my life. I know what I'll now do. From now on, I'll call myself The Tax Doctor. Thank you so much for taking time to talk to a stranger."

On a flight from Hong Kong to Singapore, I was waiting to use the restroom with several other passengers. We were in the section with four restrooms. One passenger waiting in the queue noticed my **Shift Happens!**® pin and asked what I did for a living. I explained I give seminars on customer service, write books on travel, and deliver keynote speeches on topics ranging from "Attitudes Are Caught . . . Not Taught" to "**Shift Happens!**® Coping with Change." She introduced herself as the human resources director for a large company in Singapore that could use my services. We exchanged cards and I gave her some promotional literature. Guess what? I'll return to Singapore in the near future.

## Chapter 15
### Dr. Travel Prescribes: The Zen of Flying

### ✈Travel Tip: Be a Winner

Sometimes travel is easy, sometimes it's not.

Remember, you don't have to win all the time to be a winner. Even top basketball players only make about half their shots. Even Michael Jordan doesn't make every shot. And he certainly didn't set any records when he played baseball. On the other hand, Babe Ruth was the number one strikeout king, as well as the home run king. You can't hit it out of the park every time you swing!

Most airlines have a better on-time record than that. So, even though your flight may be canceled or delayed occasionally, if you concentrate on your overall average of on-time (or near on-time) takeoffs and touchdowns, chances are you will be an overwhelming winner.

*There are only two emotions in a plane: boredom and terror.*

— Orson Welles

# 3

# Up, Up, and Away

You've made your plans, packed your bags, bought your plane tickets, and managed to get to the airport. Now it's time for you to get on the plane and, as they say onboard, "Sit back, relax, and enjoy the flight."

*Grab a stack of pillows and blankets to shove behind your back — and five Bloody Marys — and maybe you won't suffer too much.*
— William A. Liebler, back specialist

## Chapter 16
# How to Be Comfortable While Confined

That airlines are not designed for comfort is no secret. An airline's chief asset is to get you to your destination as quickly as possible. So it's up to you to make yourself as comfortable as you can under not-so-great conditions.

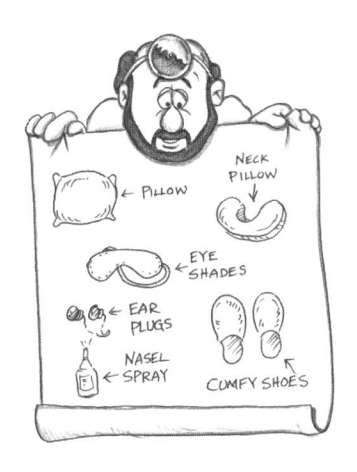

### ✈Travel Tip: Grab a Pillow

You already have a seat assignment, so chances are no one will be sitting in your seat (although it does happen once in a computer-error while). Pillows, on the other hand, are hard to come by and they can make a big difference in how you feel when you leave the aircraft.

Most airline seats, as discussed in Chapter 6, are uncomfortable. (Seats are better in Business and First Class, but still not ideal.) To counteract their poor design, put a pillow, or two, in

Part III
Up, Up, and Away

the small of your lower back. This helps reduce strain in that area. In addition, you can protect your neck by taking on board one of those inflatable U-shaped pillows. They are lightweight and easy to use. If you also want to snooze later in the flight, grab a blanket when you board. Blankets, like pillows are often in short supply.

## ✈Travel Tip: Take Slumber Gear

In addition to an inflatable neck pillow, you may want to consider taking eye shades if you want to sleep (these can also be used to discourage talkative seatmates). And take along earplugs either for sleeping or drowning out the engine sounds when you travel on the noisier, smaller, "puddle jumper" planes.

## ✈Travel Tip: Wear Loose Fitting Clothing (or None?)

Planes are often too warm or too cold. If you dress in layers, you can adjust to the cabin temperature by adding or removing clothing.

If you are tempted to take off your shoes, don't. On long flights, your feet swell and you may be unable to get your shoes on again. If you insist on removing them, make sure you put them back on at least half an hour before landing.

Of course, if it gets really hot in flight, you may want to take off all your clothes. A story in *USA Today* noted "flying naked isn't illegal." With or without clothes, women should avoid high-heeled shoes. Wear comfortable shoes on the plane. You can always change at your destination.

> *The key to relaxation while flying is to take control of the environment on an airplane. I bring my own music, my own food, and my own reading material. Before the flight takes off, I tell the flight attendants, politely, to please fill my cup with herbal tea periodically, and that, otherwise, I don't want to be disturbed.*
> — Alan Dershowitz

# Chapter 16
## Dr. Travel Prescribes: How to Be Comfortable While Confined

## ✈Travel Tip: Change Your Position

Move about the plane at least once every hour. This is good reason to ask for an aisle seat or an excellent excuse to climb over seatmates. Stand up and go to the restroom or find a place to stretch. (For specific in-your-seat exercises, see Chapter 19.)

If you are headed to the bathroom near the end of your flight, remember seat belt signs go on approximately thirty minutes before landing. Avoid the rush and long lines by using the facilities forty-five minutes or so before touchdown.

## Travel Tip: Travel and Be Well

- Wash your hands frequently. Germs are easily transmitted by touching people and handling money. Carry antiseptic wipes for those times when you can't reach a restroom.

- Ear block or ear ache? If you have a head cold or upper-respiratory congestion, cabin pressure can play havoc on your ears during takeoff and landing. If you must fly when you are unwell, take a decongestant before you leave the ground and again before the descent. But only take a decongestant if you really need one; decongestants dry out nasal passages. On longer flights, also use a nasal spray thirty to sixty minutes before landing and again during descent. If none of these are available, try one of these:

- Yawn or swallow. Hold your nostrils with your mouth closed and gently blow out. Put a few paper cocktail napkins dipped in hot water in the bottom of an airline waxed water cup (found in the restroom or near the drinking fountain). Then place the cup over your painful ear. The moist steam air can work wonders.

- Wear contact lenses? To minimize dry air eye irritation, wear eyeglasses, not contact lenses during the flight.

- Dental work? The change in cabin pressure can cause severe pain if you have had recent surgery or dental work. Don't fly within twelve hours after such medical procedures.

- Keep your tootsies up. To enhance blood circulation and to take the pressure off the back of your thighs, keep your feet elevated. You can either use your carry-on or the footrest provided in Business or First Class.

- Sound advice. Although using headphones is a great way to help pass the time or to drown out jet noise, beware. Recent research indicates the plastic ear pieces are a perfect breeding ground for bacteria that cause ear infections. Only use your own or the disinfected ones in plastic bags and only use them for thirty minutes at a time.

*Keeping your propeller balanced requires constant attention. Anytime one blade gets out of balance, no matter which one, you're in for a good shaking up.*
— Howard Putman

## ✈Travel Tip: Become a Portable Drugstore

Take along — and use — products like these: saline spray and oil or petroleum jelly to moisturize and coat the inside of your nose, saline eye drops (especially if you wear contact lenses), decongestant and chewing gum to keep your ears open, and skin moisturizer and a spray bottle of water to revive the rest of you. Consider taking Vitamin C before, during, and after your flight to help protect you against airline-related colds and flu.

## ✈Travel Tip: High and Dry

Instead of calling airplanes "airplanes," they should more accurately be called "not-much-air planes." Although airlines deny this, they are pumping in less fresh air than they used to. This, along with the extremely low-cabin humidity, can be a fertile breeding ground for colds, flu, and headaches. You can do little about a plane's ventilation system, but the following suggestions may help you minimize the effects of dry air.

## ✈Travel Tip: Flood Yourself with Fluids

- Drink plenty of water, which helps combat dehydration. Avoid alcohol, caffeine, and salty snacks. Also avoid carbonated beverages in flight; they create gas. If you are not traveling in Business or First Class where it is easier to get water whenever you want it, then carry your own bottled water. After the flight, continue to drink plenty of water.

- Keep your mouth shut. A plane's dry air, the need to shout over an engine's roar, and the bacteria-laden environment of the cabin are all less than ideal conditions for your vocal cords.

Because of this, Susan RoAne, a professional speaker who had voice problems in the past, does not say much when airborne. As the author of *How to Work a Room*, she is an advocate of chatting with fellow passengers but now, under the recommendation of her speech therapist, RoAne keeps her mouth shut. She maintains a polite and friendly manner with her seatmates while still protecting her health.

Sucking on lozenges will also help keep your mouth closed and increase saliva production.

- Fly First Class. Upgrade if you can afford it. It's more comfortable and healthier.

Not only does First Class get better food and wider seats, but the flow of fresh air can be three to seven times greater than for coach passengers. And, fewer folks are in First Class to share the air.

Although this doesn't happen often, there are times when just

Part III
Up, Up, and Away

asking to be upgraded may work. It worked for Sheila Feigelson, a humorous speaker from Ann Arbor, Michigan. "Listen," she playfully said to the gate agent, "if you need some help in filling up the First Class section, I probably could be of assistance. It would be OK with me if you want to switch my seat." They did. Sheila was traveling with colleagues who made some wisecracks as she boarded the plane before they did. To have some fun and to get back at them, she asked the flight attendant if she could do something special when her friends came on board. As they entered and headed down the aisle to their coach seats, they found Sheila relaxing in First Class and getting a temple massage from the flight attendant.

> *I don't want to sound nostalgic about the good old days, but I do miss those times when shortness of breath came from fear of flying, not oxygen deprivation.*
> — Ian Shoales

When the plane began to taxi down the runway, Sheila realized she was experiencing a professional speaker's nightmare — with an empty seat beside her, there was "No One To Talk With!" So several times during the flight, she paraded back to chat with her friends. In spite of having a First Class seat, she spent most of the flight standing in the coach section.

## ✈ Travel Tip: When You Don't Fly First Class

Even if you can't travel in the front cabin, you can do something about air quality. When you book your flight, ask your travel agent to choose an older aircraft. Newer planes recycle as much as fifty percent of the air to save on fuel costs. Most older planes (built before the mid 1980s) don't recycle. Also, avoid the Boeing 757. Not only do its three narrow seats on either side of a center aisle make this one of the most uncomfortable long-haul planes around, but a high percentage of its air is recycled. Instead, favor the Boeing 747-400. A *Consumer Reports* study said this plane has the freshest air. In addition, check how full the flight is. Fewer passengers mean

## Chapter 16
### Dr. Travel Prescribes: How to Be Comfortable While Confined

more air per person. And when they call your flight, don't make a mad dash for the plane. Air doesn't circulate much before takeoff, so delay boarding when you can.

### ✈Travel Tip: Customer Satisfaction

Many airlines take the position, "You have to fly. We are here, so get on board." Yet many airlines have readjusted their thinking after looking at the demise of Pan Am, TWA, Eastern, Contintenal, Braniff, and others, who at the time of their reorganization or closure, lost market share and revenue due to their "attitude."

When was the last time you were pampered in coach? Today, many carriers — judged by their economy service — could be called *Austere Air*. Airlines still exist that have carved out a profitable niche by offering quality service while staying out of discount fare wars.

Recently, I discovered Midwest Express. This airline is so uniformly popular with its customers that, unlike almost all other airlines, it has not been included in the Transportation Department's rankings of customer complaints because it has not received the minimum of ten complaints a year. Timothy Hoeksema, chairman and CEO, said his goal is to expand capacity at twleve to eighteen percent per year, to continue to be a good place to work, and to earn the best rate of return for stockholders. "With no debt, the constraint to our growth is how fast we can grow without losing our focus and control our quality," Hoeksema said. Milwaukee-based Midwest Express may just be the benchmark for customer service in the airline industry. As a frequent flyer, this airline offers miles of smiles.

> *There is no pleasure in traveling. I look upon it more as an occasion for spiritual testing.*
> — Albert Camus

# Part III
## Up, Up, and Away

*It isn't how much time you spend somewhere that makes it memorable; it's how you spend the time.*
— David Brenner

### ✈Travel Tip: Why Doesn't My Connecting Flight Ever Leave from the Gate Next to Where I Landed?

Not all gates can accommodate planes of every size. Because the airlines lease gates in clusters, the closest gate to where you landed may not fit the next plane you have to board. If you are switching to another airline, you must walk to a different cluster. An average plane contains passengers bound for thirty-seven different destinations, according to Randy Petersen, editor and publisher of *Inside Flyer* magazine. The real issue here is how to accommodate all those thirty-six people or groups (thirty-six plus the one that just landed). Obviously, they all cannot leave from the gate next to where they landed.

### ✈Travel Tip: Why Are My Bags the Last to Arrive at the Baggage Claim?

Baggage checked in early is usually loaded first. The only exceptions are First Class and Premium Class. Those bags are loaded last and unloaded first. This is just one more perk the airline offers their most frequent flyers. To obtain another smile at the airport become important to the airline. Frequent flyers have discovered many of the "little things" are the rewards reserved for the airlines, hotels, and car rental best customers.

### ✈Travel Tip: Why Do Airlines Assign Middle Seats or Seats Next to a Crying Child, Especially When I Book Early?

Many factors are involved in seat assignments. First, consider many of the seats are taken out of inventory and held for frequent flyers. Second, the airlines must balance the weight in the cabin, so they assign the middle of the plane first and assign seats backward from the middle to the back of the plane. After this process is complete, the airlines fill seats forward from the middle.

If you want a particular seat, do not accept the seat assignment first offered. Middle seats are usually provided only after the aisles and windows are filled. As a frequent flyer, you have preferential treatment over those passengers who aren't frequent flyers. And if you reach the upper level on traveler (1K, Platinium, and so forth) you may be upgraded. In this case, there are no middle seats, so you are assured a window or an aisle seat.

> *In America, there are two classes of travel — First Class and with children.*
> — Robert Benchley

Part III
Up, Up, and Away

*I never travel without my diary. One should always have something sensational to read.*

— Oscar Wilde

## Chapter 17
# Let Me Entertain Me

The airlines are not in the entertainment business. Their job is to get you safely from one place to another. But they know, as you know, that being cooped up in an aluminum tube hour-after-endless-hour is not much fun. So they try to keep the natives (often called *passengers*) from getting restless by distracting them with such perks as drinks, food, movies, magazines, and in-flight audio/video.

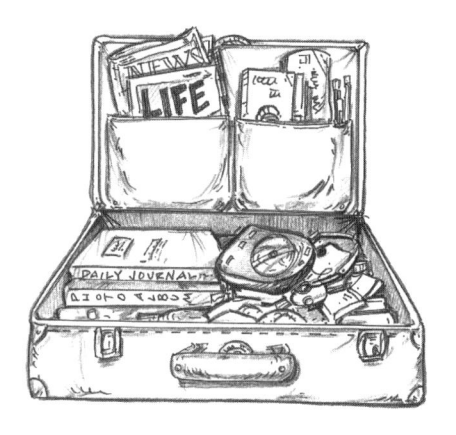

Despite what the airlines provide, preparing to entertain yourself is an excellent idea. You may have already seen the movie (three times), your seatmate may not be talkative, and the only magazine available may be *Crocheting Made Easy*. So, here to help you pass the hours, are some self-entertainment suggestions:

### ✈Travel Tip: Carry on Reading Material

Take a good book (preferably this one) to read. The Marriott Business Travel Institute suggests you take a half-finished novel. The theory is, if you are that far into the book, chances are you will dive immediately into it and the flight will pass more quickly. *USA Today* adds you should take a book with lots of pages. "Nothing is worse than finishing a novella mid-flight and being forced to read the emergency landing instructions," the newspaper says. You may want to take two books (preferably paperbacks) to give you a choice, in case one book doesn't hold your attention or your flight is delayed.

If you are taking magazines, don't carry the entire publication — it's too heavy. Instead, cut out the articles you want to read and recycle the rest.

## ✈Travel Tip: Plane Mail

Air travel is a wonderful time to catch up on unread and unanswered stuff the postal carrier delivers. I have a just-for-the-plane pile of mail (newsletters, ads, correspondence, magazine articles, and catalogs) I take along. Then I read and recycle as I go. This pile of reading also makes great material for "scrap time" — like those minutes waiting to board a flight.

Air travel is also one of the best times to answer your mail. This can be a bit more fun for those who receive your letters, as well, because envelopes frequently are postmarked from cities the recipients never knew existed.

## ✈Travel Tip: Use the Headphones

On many flights, most airlines provide in-flight audio entertainment. Make use of this entertainment. You can tune in classical music while you read. Classical music provides great background music to cut down on the jet noise, loud conversations, and noisy children.

> *Always bring a book, as protection against strangers. Magazines don't last. Newspapers from home will make you homesick and newspapers from elsewhere will remind you that you don't belong. You know how alien another paper's typeface seems.*
> — Anne Tyler

Depending on your tastes, airlines usually provide various types of music, spoken-word segments if you want to learn something new, and some of the world's greatest comedians. And if you choose the latter, because laughter helps relax muscles, you are not only passing the time, you are also getting some natural stress relief.

## ✈Travel Tip: Use Your Own Cassette or CD-ROM Player

If you are an audio tape or a CD nut, don't forget to take your favorite cassettes or CD-ROMs. These are great when your eyes get too tired to read.

Personally, I prefer spoken-word tapes. I feel as if the person on the tape is right there on the plane, speaking directly to me. Books on tape or learn-a-language tapes are also great.

If you are a nervous flyer, relaxation tapes are a godsend. Before I discovered I could follow the guided imagery on a tape, I was a white-knuckled flyer. Now I totally forget about the bumpy flight.

Do remember, though, most airlines don't allow tape recorders to be used during take-off or landing.

## ✈Travel Tip: Work

A great deal of productive work can be done on a plane. In fact, a good portion of this book was written while traveling. Patricia Fripp, an internationally known professional speaker, says that when she gets on an airplane, she considers this: "God has just given me five hours and I can do anything I want with it." Usually Fripp gathers information about her clients or works on the outlines of the speeches she plans to give.

## ✈Travel Tip: Play

Dr. Joyce Brothers says: "Many of us have to do business work on a trip, but forget to leave time for a little dessert or something you want to do very badly."

Part III
Up, Up, and Away

Remember, laptop computers are great for getting work done, but they can also be used for playing a vast variety of games. And don't forget fellow passengers — choose a game without a blaring beep.

> *Late for a flight from Duluth to a conference in Minneapolis, I arrived just in time to dash aboard. Buckling up, I noticed I was the only passenger on the 737 jet, with seven flight attendants. After take-off, I surreptitiously got permission to use the microphone: "Attention, flight crew, this is your passenger speaking."*
> — Esther Blumenfeld and Lynne Alpern

> *On some flights, to save money they don't serve any meals, just peanuts. It's working out very well as they've discovered they can serve the same bag of peanuts about three times before someone finally manages to open it.*
> — Mike Wilmot

## ✈Travel Tip: Busy Be, Happy Be

I don't knit or needlepoint, but I have seen women and men pass the time enjoyably by doing this kind of handiwork. In one case, it was also an excellent icebreaker. The flight attendant and several passengers chatted with the person doing needlepoint about the wonderful creation in progress.

On another flight, the man next to me pulled out a pile of small pieces of colored paper and proceeded to fold them into delightful Origami figures. Origami is a lightweight, easy-to-learn, fun hobby that can occupy your time and create amusement for you and others.

## ✈Travel Tip: People Watch

Whether you are delayed at the airport or cooped up in a plane, you can always entertain yourself by observing others. For exam-

# Chapter 17
## Dr. Travel Prescribes: Let Me Entertain Me

ple, here are some observations I made (providing me with almost thirty minutes of amusement) on how passengers open bags of peanuts: Businessmen typically went immediately to the Tear Here slit. They completely opened the top of the bag, tilted their heads way back and poured half the contents into their mouths. Less-aggressive types made a neat slit in the upper corner of the bag and then ate one nut at a time. These folks often stretched the consumption of the meager contents into fifteen or twenty minutes of eating pleasure. My own, not-so-scientific, study revealed more women than men used the put-your-nuts-on-the-tray approach. They dumped all the nuts onto their napkin before eating them. Then there were those people whose peanut bags could not be opened without a chain saw. They tore, they ripped, they pulled the corners with their teeth, but still the bag wouldn't open. At the end of the flight — the bag of nuts still unopened— the attendant whisked away their uneaten snack.

### ✈Travel Tip: Reach Out and Meet Someone

One of the most interesting ways to pass the time on a plane is to chat with your seatmate. By talking with the person next to you, you may meet Mr. or Ms. Wonderful, share a laugh, or possibly acquire a new business client. One poll showed a new customer contact or business relationship occurs about twenty-five percent of the time when business travelers talk with the person seated next to them.

When travel gets boring (or chaotic), remember misery loves company. Those around you are as anxious as you are to talk with someone. Become an ear for them. This helps pass the time and, who knows, you may even make a partner or a friend for life.

If your seatmate doesn't want to talk, chat with the flight attendants. Sure, they're working and can't talk for more than a few minutes at a time, but on long flights, they also get bored and may be looking for conversation. The person most people would like to sit next to on a long flight? According to one survey, it's Oprah Winfrey.

# Part III
## Up, Up, and Away

> *Never play peek-a-boo with a child on a long plane trip. There's no end to the game. Finally I grabbed him by the bib and said, "Look, it's always gonna be me!"*
> — Rita Rudner

> *Whenever I travel I like to keep the seat next to me empty. I found a great way to do it. When someone walks down the aisle and says, "Is someone sitting there?" just say, "No one except the Lord."*
> — Carol Leifer

## ✈Travel Tip: Silencing Seatmates

Chatting with the person next to you may be great, but when you want to read, sleep, or think, and the person next to you is a real talker, several ways exist to silence him or her. Comedy writer Bob Orben suggests one surefire technique to make someone stop talking. "Ask them what they paid for their ticket. And no matter what they say, tell them that you paid half and also got a coupon good for two free drinks." Orben says, "For the next three hours, the only sound you'll hear from them is the grinding of teeth."

Here are some other seatmate silencers:

- Carry a baby's pacifier with you. Pop it in your mouth and your neighbor's mouth will probably remain shut.

- Tell the person next to you you sell life insurance/raise funds for a religious cult, or are an undertaker. Conversation will probably come to a dead halt.

- Use the airline's (or your own) headphones. Put them on, but don't plug them in. Silence is assured.

- Sam Horn, president of Maui-based Action Seminars, has a four-part diplomatic silencer he calls "tactful termination." First, understand it's OK to interrupt someone when your needs are not being met. Second, say the person's name.

# Chapter 17
## Dr. Travel Prescribes: Let Me Entertain Me

Most people will pause for just a moment when they hear their names, giving you a chance to get your verbal foot in the door. Third, summarize what the person has been saying to show you've been listening. And, fourth, move on to your action statement: "I wish I had more time to chat, but I need to prepare for a meeting." The key word here is *wish*; it softens your departure.

## ✈Travel Tip: Contemplate

Some of my most creative ideas come to me when I'm flying. Sometimes I think this is because — at 30,000 feet above the earth — I'm closer to the source of all creation. Consider your time in the air as a retreat from the problems you face on the ground. Use this time for some clear thinking and long-range planning. Or, instead of constantly concerning yourself about "when are we going to get there?" try meditation.

Many people think meditation is something that takes years of grueling daily practice high on some far away mountain. On the contrary, meditation can be a quick and easy way of taking a calming inner journey or of getting your mind off something and moving it toward a more positive and relaxing place. To do this, close your eyes and either focus on your breathing or a pleasant memory, such as walking in the woods, playing with your dog, lying in a hammock, whatever. When you feel more relaxed, reopen your eyes.

> *It is easier to find a traveling companion than to get rid of one.*
> — Art Buchwald

> *On a plane, you can pick up more and better people than on any other public conveyance since the stagecoach.*
> — Anita Loos

Part III
Up, Up, and Away

## ✈Travel Tip: Sleep

When I asked Joseph Sugarman, founder of BluBlockers Sunglasses, how he made air travel more comfortable, more enjoyable, and less stressful, he said, "Sleep. Sleep. Sleep." And Sugarman is not alone.

The World Airline Entertainment Association, the organization responsible for what movies and videos are watched on planes, polled 3,697 passengers to find out what they liked to do in the air: seventy-nine percent answered they liked to sleep.

Most airlines offer in-flight movies for about $5 or less. They do not serve popcorn, but the soft drinks are free. The in-flight magazine tells you what is playing on your flight. In fact, the magazine informs you of every movie on every flight for the entire month. Recently, one of the larger airlines located in the Midwest announced it will discontinue all movies on domestic flights as a cost-cutting measure. I immediately wrote to the president and suggested he could rent pillows and blankets, charge more for hot meals instead of cold ones, and add pay-per-visit, coin-operated locks on the bathroom doors. If none of those suggestions appeal to you, forget them and get some sleep.

> *Those who enjoy being on the train (plane), and those who do not enjoy being on the train (plane), get to the same destination at the same time.*
> — John-Roger and Peter McWilliams

*There are two choices of food on airplanes: bland and tasteless.*

— Mike Shaunessy

## Chapter 18
# Travel Broadens
# (or, You Are What You Eat)

Comedians often have a field day with airline food. David Brenner, for example, notes that when flight attendants say, "You have a choice of Beef Medallions á la Rue de Paris or Chicken Kiev," what they really mean is, "Do you want shoe sole covered with pitch or bird of Chernobyl?" And Dave Barry says, "When the flight attendants ask, 'Do you want roast beef or lasagna?' they don't mean, 'do you want roast beef or do you want lasagna?' They mean, 'Do you want this dinner substance, which could be roast beef or it could be lasagna? Or possibly peat moss?'" And, finally, Erma Bombeck once declared, "No matter what you order, the entree you didn't order will look better."

Although airline food is the brunt of many jokes, it isn't as bad as it could be. Think about this: A major airline prepares about 60,000 meals a day, and the flight kitchen, like you, must deal with delays and cancellations and still get the right food onto the right flight — and all this in a limited amount of time.

With all the steps that go into the preparation and delivery of your meal, it is a miracle you get any food at all. But, if you really don't like airline food, ways exist to get more appealing, more nutritious nourishment.

## ✈Travel Tip: Eat Before You Board

One thing you can do if you detest airline meals is to eat before you fly. By eating either at home or at the airport, you have a far wider variety from which to choose than you do onboard.

## ✈Travel Tip: Check the Meal Service

The airline's meal schedule may not match your stomach's timetable — especially when you are changing time zones, be prepared.

## ✈Travel Tip: Take Your Own Food

Instead of depending on what the airlines will provide, satisfy your personal needs and tastes by packing a meal. If you choose to do this, take only foods that stay fresh for several hours without refrigeration. And, remember, it's not considered good form to take an uncooked roast beef onboard and ask the flight attendant to cook it for you!

> *You can't really blame people for being concerned about the safety of flying. Who in their right mind would want their last meal to be airline food?*
> — Bob Orben

Linda Prout, nutritionist at the Claremont Resort and Spa in Oakland, California, likes to take hard-boiled eggs along when she travels. She says they make a nutritious, easy-to-carry, quick meal. Prout also points out that in Eastern thinking, eggs fall under the contractive category of food that draws nervous energy out of the body (a benefit many of us can use when airborne).

# Chapter 18
## Dr. Travel Prescribes: Travel Broadens (or, You are What You Eat)

### ✈Travel Tip: Order a Special Meal

Most major airlines offer something many airline passengers don't know about. You can get a special meal and you needn't be a vegetarian or on a diet. All you must do is request a special meal from six to twenty-four hours before your flight. In addition, special meals also make you feel special. Don't you like to hear your name called out over the intercom when the flight attendant is looking for the person who ordered the special meal? Frequently, too, a meal you order to replace the usual fare contains a small card on the tray reading, "Welcome aboard. We have prepared this meal especially for you. Enjoy the flight!" Now doesn't that make you feel like you are getting First Class treatment despite the fact you're flying coach?

Even for the seasoned jet setter, who is often served the same kind of meal, a special meal can be a nice change of pace.

Here, in three categories, are some of the special meals you can request:

- ✓ Religious: Hindu, Kosher, Moslem
- ✓ Special Diet: Diabetic, low-fat, low-sodium, lactose-restricted meals
- ✓ Other: Fruit plate, seafood, vegetarian, child's (hot dog or hamburger) meals

While some of these may not make your palate sing with joy, they do offer another option and, particularly in the case of the fruit plate, a healthier choice than standard air fare. If you don't order a special meal, at least avoid entrees with heavy sauces. They are high in fat and calories. If available, select something broiled or baked instead.

Part III
Up, Up, and Away

## ✈Travel Tip: Drink to Your Health

### Healthy:

The atmosphere on a plane is drier than the air in the Sahara Desert. I don't know how accurate this is, but I have experienced how dry the air is on an airplane. Once a flight attendant spilled some red wine on me and cleaned it up with sparkling soda water. I thought I'd have to sit there with a wet suit for hours, but it was completely dry within ten minutes. Drinking lots of water to prevent dehydration has previously been discussed in this book, but this is such an important point, it's worth mentioning again.

> *If it weren't for airlines, we'd be up to our necks in honey-roasted peanuts.*
> — Gene Perret

### Not So Healthy:

- Alcoholic beverages: Alcohol dehydrates you at high altitudes and you feel the effects of alcohol more quickly. "A glass of wine in the air," notes one health consultant, "is comparable to three glasses on the ground."

- Drinks and foods with caffeine: Coffee, tea, cola, and chocolate disrupt your sleep both at home and on the plane. Avoid consuming any caffeine, beginning the day before your flight.

- Anything with bubbles: Pressure in plane causes things to swell (including your feet and intestines).

Chapter 18
Dr. Travel Prescribes: Travel Broadens (or, You are What You Eat)

## ✈Travel Tip: Don't Eat the Nuts

Peanuts are high in fat grams. In addition, the salt on nuts increases dehydration in an already dry atmosphere. Instead of the peanuts, pack your own snacks. Here are some suggestions for lightweight, nutritious, and easy-to-carry foods to take with you:

- ✓ Fresh fruit (oranges, apples and bananas travel well)
- ✓ Fruit strips or dried fruit
- ✓ Protein or Granola bars (sugarless/fat free)
- ✓ Whole grain rolls, crackers, or unsalted, unbuttered popcorn

In addition to being healthier, these snacks can be used as a supplement if your special meal wasn't boarded or when your eating times are altered by delays and time-zone changes. In any case, the snacks will tide you over until a real meal comes along.

## ✈Travel Tip: First Class Meals

Don't fly First Class for the meal service. You can eat at the best gourmet restaurant in the city where you depart or arrive for much less. While traveling to London, my friend Michelle and I experienced a wonderful meal service, which included smoked salmon, Dom Perignon champagne, choice of rainbow trout, Beef Wellington, or roast duck for the entree. Michelle had never flown First Class before. She was totally impressed with the service and food selection. In fact, part of the negative contemplation of leaving London was reduced by the thought of the meal service back to the U.S. Upon boarding, we found ourselves alone in the First Class cabin. The flight attendant poured the champagne and read us the menu instead of handing it to us. We weren't really hungry, so we started with the caviar, smoked salmon, and then more champagne. The flight attendant made up the entire presentation on the serving cart and placed it next to my seat. "When you run out, ring the bell," she said. For the next six hours, we consumed all the caviar and Dom Perignon onboard. We gave the meals to the crew. Clearly a win-win situation for everyone — and what fun! The next morning, I stayed in bed because of Dom Lag.

> Delta Airlines says it will save $1.4 million in food and labor costs by elimination the decorative piece of lettuce served under the vegetables on in-flight meals.
> — *Playboy*

## ✈Travel Tip: Don't Eat, Period

Because the pressurized conditions on a plane cause stress on your body, eating less is better for you. In fact, some studies have found that eating less in general can prolong your life. Unless you are in First Class on an overseas flight, you won't miss the meal. And even in First Class, once the caviar and champagne have been passed, your meal can run the gamut from well-above average to merely passable because the final preparation is done by a flight attendant, who may or may not know how to prepare the meal. Sometimes meals are over- or undercooked, presented in tin foil trays instead of on a plate, and offered without any indication of what the meal contains in the way of sauces, sugars, or fat.

*I do three special exercises on a plane: Skip meals, lift spirits, and jump to conclusions.*

— Doc Blakely

## Chapter 19
# Be Fit While You Sit

On a long plane trip, your body goes on a sit-down strike. Muscle tone deteriorates, your circulation slows down, your oxygen supply is cut back, and the lack of muscle movement prevents blood in your lower legs from returning to your heart. The results are swollen ankles and clotting in the veins, which can lead to more serious problems.

Dr. Stephen Yarnall, a heart specialist in Edmonds, Washington, calls this *Sitting Syndrome*. To prevent it, Dr. Yarnall recommends you wiggle *your toes* and fidget in your seat. "Sitting Syndrome is virtually never seen in fidgety kids," Yarnall says.

One airline was so concerned about the immobility of passengers during their long-haul, intercontinental flights, they developed both a *Fitness in the (Ch)air* booklet and a video called *Flyrobics*. The twelve-minute program and pamphlet show passengers movements to aid muscle toning. Most of these movements are inconspicuous, take little time, and are easy to do. Several follow, along with some other fit-while-you-sit exercises.

## ✈Travel Tip: Tense and Relax

One of the simplest, least conspicuous, and most beneficial exercises you can do while seated is to tighten and relax every muscle in your body systematically . Try it with your legs first: tighten the toes on your left foot and then let go. Tighten your left calf muscle and then relax. Next, tighten the left thigh muscle and then relax. Finally, complete the left side by doing the same with your buttocks. Repeat several times and then do the same on the right side.

## ✈Travel Tip: Incorporate Some Isometrics

Once an hour, press your hands down on the arm rests. Hold for fifteen seconds. Relax and repeat. Do the same with your legs pressed against the floor.

While standing, find a wall, (probably near an exit or the restroom), put both palms out at about chest level and press your weigh on the wall, as if you are doing push-ups, but without moving up and down.

## ✈Travel Tip: Let 'er Roll

- Head rolls — Drop your head forward and then gently roll it backward to a count of eight. First do this clockwise and then counterclockwise several times.

> *The only aerobic exercise anyone gets on a plane is disengaging oneself from the jaws of the folding door of the restroom that threatens to digest you.*
> — Erma Bombeck

- Shoulder rolls — Move your shoulders in both front and

backward circular motions. If you want, you can alternate this with shoulder shrugs. Lift your shoulders toward your ears and then let them drop, repeating the process several times.

- Foot rolls — Rotate each ankle in large circles every half hour, first in one direction and then in the other.

- Eye rolls — With your eyes closed, pretend your eyes are following the hands of a clock. Start at twelve — and to a count of four — move them slowly past three, six, and nine, and then back to twelve. Repeat counterclockwise. To complete this exercise, rub the palms of your hands together rapidly until they are warm. Then cup your palms over your eyes. Allow the warmth of your hands to soothe away fatigue.

## ✈Travel Tip: Stretch It Out

Dr. Jerry Teplitz, from Virginia Beach, Virginia, suggests the following stretching exercises when confined in a plane seat:

- Stretch your arms above your head and rotate from the waist. Circle around one way and then the other way for about half a dozen times. Lean to the right and then lean to the left for another half-dozen stretches.

- Lift your leg up and, with your fingers intertwined, put your hands around your kneecap, and then pull your leg toward your chest. Keep your back straight, hold, and then drop your leg down. Hold and then drop your leg down again. Do this with each leg about half a dozen times.

- Lean as far forward in your seat as you can. Then lean backward, tilt your head with your chest out. Come back down again as far as you can go, and then lean backward again. Repeat several times.

Dr. Betsy Morscher, the spa consultant, recommends several exercises that, in addition to getting your circulation going, may also turn-on or turn-off your seatmate:

- Jog in place. Put on the headphones and tune in to an upbeat station. Then raise your heels alternately as high as possible. At the same time, move your arms in a bent position and rock rhythmically forward and back.
- Lean back and open your mouth as wide as possible. Close your mouth. Repeat several times.
- Reach up repeatedly with one hand and then the other.
- Give yourself a hug. Repeat nine more times.

> *Breathing increases the supply of oxygen to the body.*
> *Stretching moves that oxygen around*
> — John-Roger and Peter McWilliams

## ✈Travel Tip: Get Out of Your Seat

The first, and perhaps easiest, activity, to help you be fit while you sit, is not to sit for too long. Get out of your seat and parade up and down the aisle at least once an hour (providing the flight attendants' carts don't make the aisle an obstacle course).

Once out of your seat, you can also do some simple reach-the-sky stretches or try some knee squats. Both help to keep your muscles toned and get your circulation moving. They can easily be done near the exits, where there is more room, or in the restroom (providing, of course, no long line is waiting).

Remember, you will be sitting in a very narrow seat. Next to you could be a larger person, a crying baby, or a super model. In each case, you want to be responsive to your own needs. The body needs to be exercised and flying is no exception. Take the time to spend ten minutes to exercise on each flight of two hours or more. This also helps pass the time.

## ✈Travel Tip: Get Exercise Rubber Bands

I travel with large rubber bands. I use them to stretch, workout, and play games. I try to see how long I can hold the rubber band stretched to the fullest extent. I put one on my foot and do bicep curls. I put a rubber band around my tray table and pull it back to my chest. It's fun and keeps your circulation moving. My fellow passengers even enjoy the antics and ask to try the rubber bands themselves. Now you've found something to break the ice. Remember to think about a breaking rubber band and its potential damage. Don't stretch it so far as to test its strength. Test your own strength instead!

> *As far as physical activity goes, jet travel is like a sandwich. On the outside are spurts of aerobic activity at odd hours before and after flights. In the center is the spread of static conformity in seats confining and tight.*
>
> — Diana Fairchild

Part III
Up, Up, and Away

*Don't be afraid of flying. It's crashing you should be afraid of.*

— Groucho Marx

## Chapter 20
# A Crash Course in Airline Safety

If you have a fear of flying, you are not alone.

A Gallop poll found that forty-four percent of Americans dread getting on a plane. This fear is so great, one psychologist estimates three–four percent of the population equates flying with going to the electric chair. *aviophobia* (the fear of flying) is, according to *USA Today,* the second biggest phobia following public speaking.

Airborne anxiety plays no favorites. It can attack anyone, including the rich and famous. Three-time heavyweight champion Mohammed Ali says, "The only thing in the world I'm scared of is flying." Joining him are such luminaries as actresses Maureen Stapleton, Glenda Jackson, and Joanne Woodward, actor Sam Shepard, entertainer/actress Cher, former President Ronald Reagan, comedian Bob Newhart, movie critic Gene Shallit, singer Aretha Franklin, and football coach/broadcaster John Madden.

What makes a natural fear of flying go away? My first realization was if I wanted to continue in the professional speaking business, I would have to fly. I could not do a program in Kissamee, Florida

Part III
Up, Up, and Away

one day and Kalamazoo, Michigan the next day without air travel. The second realization that partially changed my feelings about flying is the statistics. Did your know flying is nineteen to thirty times safer than driving and ten times safer than train travel? In fact, you are more likely to die of a bee sting or to be hit by a baseball at a major league game than to die in an airplane crash!

Although the facts were impressive, my fear remained. What really got me over my fear was the awareness of a flying paradox. Although I lacked control about nearly everything connected to flying, I did have complete control over my reactions. So I began to use many of the techniques in this book, such as deep breathing, relaxation tapes, and using my sense of humor, to overcome my fear of flying. And the more I flew, the more comfortable I became.

I also found a wonderful retrospective story in Eric Johnson's, *A Treasury of Humor*, (Prometheus Books, Buffalo, NY) who said if you are afraid to fly, you wouldn't have stepped on a plane in the 1930s. The following instructions are from one of the first manuals for flight attendants:

1. Keep the clock and altimeter wound up.
2. Carry a railroad timetable in case the plane is grounded.
3. Warn the passengers against throwing their cigars and cigarettes out the windows.
4. Keep an eye on passengers when they go to the restroom to be sure they don't mistakenly go out the emergency exit.

> *Flying is the second greatest thrill known to man.*
> *Landing is first.*
> —Anonymous

Over the years, I have learned to decrease my fear of flying. Here are some techniques you can try.

# Chapter 20
## Dr. Travel Prescribes: A Crash Course in Airline Safety

### ✈Travel Tip: Easing the Fear

- Stop those thoughts.

Your mind can either be your greatest asset in overcoming your fear of flying or your greatest enemy. When the plane encounters some turbulence, for example, instead of thinking about every bump, consider all the people at amusement parks who are spending their money to be bounced around on rides. Image the joy children have on roller coasters and vividly see their exuberant smiling faces in your mind.

- Snap out of it.

Before you get on a plane, put a rubber band on your wrist. When you have a negative thought about flying, snap the rubber band as a reminder to change your way of thinking.

- Distract yourself.

During the flight, divert your attention away from your fears with a good book, a good conversation, or the in-flight movie. You may even want to do something totally outrageous.

For example, Mary Lou Moore from Springfield, Ohio, had never flown before. She was anxious and nervous about it, so she got her friend, Chris Garrett, to join her. They thought if they got loud and obnoxious, everything would be all right. So they dressed as two outspoken bag ladies and renamed themselves Maxine and Tildie. Using overstuffed shopping bags as carry-ons, they created lots of laughs. Metal detectors beeped because of their wristwatch covered arms, passengers used airsickness bags to write down their names and addresses, and they even gave the captain a breathe test to make sure he was sober. Their delightful antics were rewarded with champagne and, in the words of Mary Lou (a.k.a. Maxine), "If we were some kind of royalty, we wouldn't have been treated better." Of course, Mary Lou lost her fear of flying.

- Chat with others.

Part III
Up, Up, and Away

If possible, greet the captain and crew. Talk with flight attendants and your seatmates. Making contact with other people can help you feel less alone in your fear. In addition, it gives you an icebreaker. Always introduce yourself to those near you. It's amazing how many new friends and business contacts I've made over the years just by saying "Hello."

- Avoid flying on airlines in financial trouble — they could be cutting corners on maintenance.
- Educate yourself.

Learn about the inner workings of aircraft and flight safety, so you'll feel more secure. Here are some examples:

*Equipment* — A commercial jet plane can land even when some of its engines are not operating. They also have collision-avoidance alarms, which sound when one plane is flying too close to another. In addition, airlines use sophisticated onboard radar equipment and meteorologists to monitor the weather. Whenever possible, pilots try to avoid bad weather to assure smoother and safer flights.

> *It's a simple theory. Matter is lighter than air. You see, the motors, they pull the plane forward and they cause a draft, and then it taxis faster down the field, and the motors go faster, and the whole plane vibrates, and then, when there's enough of a draft and a vacuum created, the plane rises off the runway into the air. From then on, it's a miracle. I don't know what keeps it up.*
> — Mel Brooks

# Chapter 20
## Dr. Travel Prescribes: A Crash Course in Airline Safety

*Sounds* — Just like a car, planes make certain noises when operating. These noises are normal and part of the proper workings of the aircraft. Different sounds occur during takeoff, when airborne, and during landing. In addition, some sounds only occur during specific maneuvers. For example, when snow is on the ground, after take-off, wheels are often lowered and raised again to shake loose any snow that may have accumulated while going down the runway. Also, as with different models of cars, not all types of aircraft sound the same. Of course, no way exists to become familiar with all sounds of all aircraft, but the more you fly, the more familiar you become with the sounds and the more comfortable you may feel.

*Turbulence* — Just as cars encounter potholes, planes also fly over atmospheric potholes of choppy air, which creates a bumpy ride occasionally. But planes are built like battleships and can withstand strong turbulence.

*Safety* — One study, by a statistics professor at M.I.T., showed that a person who took one domestic jet flight every single day could go on average more than 29,000 years before succumbing to a fatal accident.

- Accept your anxiety.

One woman told me her first flight was incredibly bumpy. Now, every time she flies, she worries if the flight is smooth, something is wrong — perhaps the plane isn't moving and it will fall out of the sky. For her, a bumpy ride signifies movement and safety. Part of any phobia is its irrationality. Honor your fear, but also acknowledge it can be conquered.

- Trust your gut.

Donna Hartley, an international motivational speaker from Tahoe City, California, dreamed six times she was going to crash. Despite this recurring nightmare, Donna boarded the plane, which exploded on takeoff and burned to the ground. Donna survived the crash using some of the following techniques. And she continues to fly regularly. But her message to others now is to listen to your intuition. "Not just the little nervousness about going somewhere, but ask yourself, what is the feeling from? If you don't want to see someone on the other end or you're afraid of work, it's one thing. But if you get a strong sense something is wrong with the flight, technically or otherwise, that's another thing."

- Aviophobia can be cured. Check out the fearful flier programs run by some airlines or by private companies.

## ✈Travel Tip: Increase Your Survival Odds

- Watch the safety video and review the emergency instruction cards found in the seat pockets.
- Count the rows from your seat to the nearest exit. If heavy smoke and/or darkness make seeing difficult, at least you can feel your way to an exit.
- Locate at least two exits. Sometimes one exit gets blocked in a crash.

> *I say to myself, "Well, I'm strapping myself into the seat. Because if I wasn't strapped into the seat, there's a very good chance I will fall out of this seat. If the plane came to a sudden stop, like against a mountain.*
> — Shelley Berman

- Travel with a smoke hood.

In an aircraft fire, smoke inhalation is the most serious threat to survival. Smoke hoods filter out smoke and toxic gases and they provide extra breathing time. They are compact, lightweight, and available from safety catalogs.

- Consider selecting an aisle seat.

Choose an aisle seat no further than three rows from an exit and in the rear of the plane. Predicting what part of the aircraft will be

## Chapter 20
### Dr. Travel Prescribes: A Crash Course in Airline Safety

damaged in a crash is impossible, but some studies show the rear of the plane is the safest. In addition, aisle seats near an exit give you access to quicker evacuation.

- Wear clothing made of natural fibers.

Wear cotton or wool clothing that covers most of your body. Avoid wearing synthetics — nylon stockings, for example, melt at high heat. Also, wear flat-heeled shoes. High heels can be a hazard when you're trying to move fast.

- Carry a handkerchief.

If you have a hanky or something similar, you can cover your nose and mouth in case of smoke, if you don't have a smoke hood.

- Remove headphones and take pens or pencils out of your pockets during takeoff and landing.

- Stay low if there's a fire . . . maybe.

Staying under the smoke is important, but it's more important to stay focused, stay calm, and do what you must do to escape. Donna Hartley survived a fiery plane crash by not staying low. Because the aisles were crowded with people, Donna walked on the armrests of the seats to get to the nearest exit.

- Don't automatically go forward. The best exits may actually be behind you.

- Avoid alcoholic drinks. They slow down your reflexes.

- Accidents happen most often during takeoffs and landings. Book nonstop flights for fewer takeoffs and landings.

- Choose the safer aircraft.

*Condé Nast Traveler* magazine conducted a poll of pilots working for major U.S. airlines. They selected the Boeing 727 and 757 as the safest narrow body jets and the 747 the safest wide body.

Part III
Up, Up, and Away

> *Ground Hug Day — celebrated by people afraid of flying.*
> — Mensa Bulletin

> *I count my blessings and do my best. I have faith that the Almighty Pilot takes care of the rest.*
> — Diana Fairchild

- Choose a major carrier or a regional airline.

Larger carriers have a better safety record than smaller commuter airlines.

- Choose a newer model plane over an older one.

Newer model planes are less likely to have metal fatigue or other age-related problems.

- "Over seventy-one percent of the people who die in survivable crashes, die after their aircraft comes to a complete stop," says Charles Chittum of the F.A.A. In most cases, the reason is passengers did not pay attention to the flight attendant's briefing, they did not locate the nearest exit, and they did not read the briefing card in the seat back pocket.
- Take a pocket flashlight and pocketknife.
- Take medications, such as insulin, which you must take every day. Medical attention may take hours to get to you if you are not critically injured.
- Wear natural fibers and tightly knit fabrics.

Natural fibers neither catch fire nor melt. Wear long pants and long sleeves so your skin is covered. I also suggest wearing a hat. A hat provides protection if drippings fall on your head. Do not dress like you are taking a long bus ride. Be comfortable, but remember, you can control your survival rate by staying alert, dressing proactively, and keeping your head clear.

## Chapter 20
## Dr. Travel Prescribes: A Crash Course in Airline Safety

## ✈Travel Tip: Stay Alert, Dress Properly, Know the Location of the Nearest Exit

Listen to the briefing and read the safety card. In case of an accident, leave your personal belongings behind. Do not inflate your life vest, if applicable, until after you leave the plane. Above all, remain calm! "Passengers who are prepared to survive a survivable accident usually do," says Charles Chittum.

- Keep your seat belt fastened.

As flight attendants always announce on the plane, "Keep your seat belt fastened low and tight around your hips." And keep it loosely fastened about you while you're seated . . . for the entire duration of the flight.

> *I was on an airplane. The pilot came running down the aisle with a parachute strapped to his back. He said, 'Don't be alarmed, but we're having a little trouble with the landing gear. I'm gonna run on ahead and warn them at the airport.'*
>
> — Slappy White

Part III
Up, Up, and Away

*Jet lag is nature's way of making you look like your passport photo.*

— Linda Perret

## Chapter 21

# Jet Lag: Eat, Wash, or Smell It Away?

As with remedies for baldness, so dozens of factual, fictional, and fanciful antidotes exist for jet lag. You can try to get rid of jet lag by fasting, by feasting, by feasting and fasting, by sleeping, or by staying awake. One cure I read about advised passengers to wear brown paper grocery bags inside their shoes.

Do any of these methods work? Yes and no. Some don't work at all (like the brown paper bags), some work some of the time, and some only work in combination with others. Even if some of the remedies don't completely cure jet lag, they do curtail it. Try some of the following techniques to find out which jet lag cure works best for you.

### What Is Jet Lag?

If you suffer from jet lag, you are not alone. One study showed as many as ninety-four percent of long-haul fliers experienced some form of it. Other research indicated even flight attendants are not immune. Jet lag includes such physical symptoms as fatigue, insomnia, disorientation, swelling limbs, ear/nose/eye irritations, headaches, irregularity, and light-headedness.

In other words, your body is out of whack. So much so, it can impede both your physical and mental performance. Greg Louganis, world champion Olympic diver, blamed jet lag for accidentally hitting his head on the diving platform during the 1979 Olympic trials. John Foster Dulles, former American Secretary of State, blamed jet lag for his poor judgment after he flew to Egypt to conduct negotiations on the Aswan Dam.

Jet lag occurs because changes in time zones confuse the body's twenty-four-hour inner clock known as *circadian rhythms*. If you live in California and you fly to New York, the time is three hours later. If you are now on the East Coast and you are ready to go to bed at your usual time of 11 P.M., your body knows it is only 8 P.M. You will have a hard time getting to sleep. In the morning, when you arise at 6 A.M., your body says, wait a minute, it's only 3 A.M.

For each time zone you cross, your body can take as long as one day to adjust. The length of your flight doesn't determine how much jet lag you may experience; instead it's how many time zones you've gone through. Jet lag seems to be worse flying eastward. Traveling north to south, within the same time zone, on the other hand, produces no jet lag.

In addition, your general health, personal habits, and age play a part in your susceptibility to jet lag. For example, babies are scarcely bothered by it. For adults, being well-rested can help reduce jet lag symptoms while overeating, smoking, and drinking alcohol can make the symptoms worse.

> *A drug called Melatonin has been used effectively on sheep, but how many sheep do you know who are frequent flyers?*
>
> — Erma Bombeck

## Chapter 21
### Dr. Travel Prescribes: Jet Lag: Eat, Wash, or Smell it Away?

### ✈Travel Tip: Sleep-Away Jet Lag

If you are flying from the West Coast to the East Coast, adjust your sleep time before you leave on your trip. If your normal bedtime is midnight, then three nights before you travel, go to sleep at 11 P.M. Two days before you travel, retire at 10 P.M. And the night before your trip, try to go to sleep at 9 P.M. (midnight on the East Coast).

On international travel, seasoned passengers either book overnight flights when heading east, so they can sleep for most of the flight, or flights that arrive at night, so they can go to bed at their destination. (Take an eye mask to enhance sleep on the plane and at your destination.)

### ✈Travel Tip: Change-Your-Watch Cure

Adapt to your new time zone as quickly as possible, especially at meal and sleep times.

On the plane: Change your watch to your destination time zone. Sleep on the plane if it's bedtime in your arrival city; stay awake if it isn't bedtime.

When you arrive: Don't think about what time it is back home. Resist taking a nap because naps delay adjustment to your new time zone. If you must nap, make it a brief one. If you are on a business trip and need to keep track of the time in your home office, a watch with two time zones may work for you. As a very frequent traveler, I must have a home time to understand what my body is telling me. Eat, sleep, exercise, whatever. Even though I may be unable to accept that time has changed, I try to keep the same schedule when out of town — especially on bicoastal trips where the time zones are either two hours earlier or two hours later. Then the return to my home time is not so dramatic.

### ✈Travel Tip: Pop-a-Pill Cure

Melatonin, an over the counter product, is being touted as the new miracle jet-lag pill. Melatonin is a substance naturally produced in humans at night. Supposedly, it tricks the body into resetting the natural sleep/awake cycle. If you take Melatonin in the morning, it delays your body clock and enables you to stay up later. If you take Melatonin at night, it encourages sleep. After trying it several times at night, my sleep was still irregular, although deeper, but my dreams were more bizarre!

Another pill on the market, called No Jet-Lag, comes from New Zealand (distributed by Flemington Pharmaceuticals in the U.S.). The tablets are made of all natural homeopathic remedies and should be chewed every two hours after takeoff.

> *Traveling is anxious work. The trouble with "Getting Away From It All" is you, indeed, get away from it all — all those background comforts of home — as well as from the unconscious ease with familiar smells, sounds, and cultural patterns.*
> — Robert Fulghum

> *Here's another way to describe jet lag: it's like getting off a not so merry-go-round only to discover you're not even at an amusement park!*
> — Diana Fairchild

## ✈Travel Tip: Supplement-Away Jet Lag

Some researchers have found certain vitamins are depleted in an airplane's unnatural atmosphere. This could be another contributor to jet lag. To counteract this, one book recommends taking Vitamin B12 two weeks before and one week after a flight. Still another source suggests doses of time-released Vitamin C (1,000 milligrams) starting the day before departure and stopping a day after the return home. In addition, on a long flight, potassium can be drained from the body by lack of activity. Counteract this deficiency by drinking orange juice or eating a banana.

# Chapter 21
## Dr. Travel Prescribes: Jet Lag: Eat, Wash, or Smell it Away?

### ✈Travel Tip: Eat-Away Jet Lag

For several years, a popular and complicated eating regime existed to overcome jet lag. This involved alternating periods of feasting and fasting several days before the flight. Supposedly, even former President Ronald Reagan and Nancy followed it during their summit travels. One military study, however, found the diet to be worthless.

This is worth remembering: protein-rich meals stimulate wakefulness and high-carbohydrate meals promote sleep. Also, once you arrive at your destination, drink beverages with caffeine to help you stay awake until bedtime and/or to help you wake up in the morning. And eat high-fiber foods to fight constipation and avoid fatty foods, which contribute to your sluggishness.

If you have Internet access, you can discover great eateries in cities around the U.S. Look up the Dr. Travel Web site at http://www.doctor-travel.com under the heading of "What to Eat When Traveling."

### ✈Travel Tip: Don't Eat Cure

Some frequent fliers recommend you don't eat anything on a flight. Their reasoning is the body is already stressed by a plane's hostile atmosphere and eating only adds one more thing for it to combat.

Like some of you, though, I don't function well without sustenance, so I recommend you do eat in moderation on the plane.

> *I have jet lag. That's when you arrive and your luggage is in better shape than you are.*
> — Gene Perret

### ✈Travel Tip: Let-There-Be-Light Cure

We all know plants need light to survive. Bright light may be the way to survive jet lag, but some controversy exists about which kind of light works best — natural, artificial, morning, or afternoon.

One hotel in Germany, for example, has installed a jet lag treatment room equipped with artificial high-intensity lighting. Some jet lag light-cure advocates, on the other hand, suggest you must get outdoors: five hours of sunlight a day are recommended. And two Harvard scientists say for light to be effective against jet lag, it must be specific: avoid light in the morning and maximize it in the afternoon.

## ✈Travel Tip: Exercise-Away Jet Lag

A German study found sedentary passengers suffered more jet lag than those who walk or exercise. Exercise, both in the air and upon arrival, will circulate your blood and help rejuvenate you.

When you're at the airport, forget those moving sidewalks. Instead, walk to your plane, walk during layovers, walk when your plane is delayed. In addition to helping you adjust to flying stagnation, walking also helps time fly.

## ✈Travel Tip: Wash-Away Jet Lag

Drink it, splash your face with it, inhale it, spray yourself with it, bathe in it. The dry atmosphere of planes puts a tremendous stress on your body. Counteract this by drenching yourself with water, inside and out.

One authority, who thinks dehydration is the main culprit of jet lag, recommends you drink two glasses of water before getting on the plane and one or more liters in flight. An added bonus of keeping your body well-hydrated is it helps you stay well. Dry membranes are more susceptible to infection. To understand how important water is to our physical well-being, remember you can live for weeks without food, but you can live only several days without water.

Bob Ginsburg, a healer who works with people's energy, suggests another jet lag water cure. After his flight, Bob takes a special cleansing bath to rid his body of toxins accumulated while flying. He travels with one pound each of iodized sea salt and baking soda and dissolves it in warm water. While this may sound unusual, think how refreshing a dip in the salt-rich ocean is and how frequently salt water heals minor cuts and scratches.

> *Discoveries are often made by not following instructions, by going off the main road, by trying the untried. Each trip should result in finding at least one new discovery and savoring the experience.*
> — Jim Feldman

> *. . . people don't take trips — trips take people.*
> — John Steinbeck

## ✈Travel Tip: Smell-Away Jet Lag

One foreign airline believes jet lag can be eased with smell. This airline's Upper Class passengers are supplied with an After-Flight Regulator Kit. Inside is a bottle of Awake and a bottle of Asleep. Each bottle contains a blend of fifty fragrances, which either stimulate or soothe the senses. When added to the bath or shower, these scents either perk up passengers or put them to sleep.

## ✈Travel Tip: Think-Away Jet Lag

The bottom line for beating jet lag is to realize it is not only a state of body, but it is also a state of mind. Al Michaels, the play-by-play announcer for *Monday Night Football*, has traveled millions of miles in his career. Michaels says he has tried all kinds of crazy things to deal with jet lag, but only one thing that really works. "The key is to get it out of your mind. The less you think about it, the better off you are."

Part IV
Upon Arrival

> **The best car safety device is a rear view mirror with a cop in it.**

*A sign in an Ugly Duckling Car Rental location:*

# 4

# Upon Arrival

*Imagine your mind like a light switch. Flick off dark thoughts, turn on ones that brighten your mood.*
— Letitia Baldridge

Part IV
Upon Arrival

> *Whenever I rent a car, to cut down on the mileage rate,*
> *I back up everywhere.*
> — Woody Allen

The purpose of this book is to show you how to be a happier, healthier, and more hearty airline passenger. But, unless you are headed home, the hassles of travel don't stop when you get off the plane. You still have to deal with such things as car rentals, hotels/motels, eating out, and so forth. The following chapters focus on how to keep your comfort up (and your costs down) when you're out of town.

*Dear Miss Piggy,
My car engine turns over, but it won't start. I've checked the plugs, the points, the condenser, the coil, the distributor, and I even sprayed carburetor cleaner in the carb, but no dice. What gives?*

*Dear Stuck,
It sounds to me like your car is broken. If you need it soon, I would get it fixed.*
     — Miss Piggy, *Miss Piggy's Guide to Life*

# Chapter 22
# Renting a Car

## ✈Travel Tip: When You Need Wheels

- If your plane is going to be late, call the rental car company and tell them. Some will only hold reservations a few hours.

- Renting from off-site car rental operators is usually less expensive than renting from on-site companies at the airport.

Make certain you know how to get back to the site to return the car, though. Off-site car rental companies often are in out-of-the-way locations.

- Ask for a car with the lowest mileage; it's newer and safer.

- Some companies charge for an extra driver — even a spouse. Ask before you rent.

- One-way rentals often carry a drop-off charge. Shop around before you book.

- Unlimited mileage may not always be unlimited. Some companies have geographic boundaries, while others may have a cap on how far you can go.

- To weed out high-risk drivers, car-rental agencies are now blacklisting drivers who have been cited for speeding or other moving violations. If in doubt, have your record checked before you reserve the car, not at the rental counter. If you wait, it may be too late.

- Before you purchase the extra collision and loss waivers, find out if your existing car policy or credit card covers it. If you own a car, your personal auto insurance probably covers you. Check with your insurance agent or reread your policy.

If you don't own a car and your credit card doesn't provide you with renter's insurance, take the collision damage waiver, which covers damage to the rental car and supplementary liability coverage.

- "Don't assume the gas tank is full because the needle is on *F*," says Jon LeSage, executive editor of *Auto Rental News.*

If you return the car with the fuel gauge needle anywhere to the left of *F*, you will be charged for the missing gas, often $3 a gallon or more. If you are in doubt, make the rental company fill up the car again prior to your leaving or have the exact gauge reading marked on the contract and signed by the guard who lets you out of the parking lot.

# Chapter 22
## Dr. Travel Prescribes: Renting a Car

*Have you noticed? Anyone going slower than you is an idiot, and anyone going faster than you is a moron.*
— George Carlin

- Avoid paying exorbitant refueling fees. Return your rental car with a full tank of gas.

- If the car agency tries to persuade you to upgrade to a bigger car than the one you reserved, refuse. Often that's all they have available, so you'll get a better car at the original price anyway.

- If you have a reservation and the agency does not have a car to give you, ask if they will pay the difference if you rent from another company at a higher rate.

- If you're a member of AAA, tell them. You'll get a discount. Also ask about weekend or weekly (five days or more) specials.

- You are in a strange car, in a strange town. For safety sake, don't drive out of the rental parking lot without knowing your route.

- Join the car rental company's frequent renter club. In many cases, you get free upgrades and preferential treatment. Make sure you bring your number or identification card. Save your confirmation number on a Post-it Note™ and attach the note to your plastic ID card. If the rental company has no record of your rental request, this will help.

- Rent your car from the hotel and not from the airport locations. In many cases, you can take the shuttle to the hotel where you are staying and retrieve your car there. You will eliminate at least one more loading and unloading of your luggage, another tip, and other delays. If you plan to stay at this hotel frequently, introduce yourself to the car rental clerk. This technique can result in no charge upgrades, a few extra hours use of the car at no additional charge, and the increased possibility your car will be held if your plane is delayed.

- Realize extra charges are now being added at major airports.

Part IV
Upon Arrival

Phoenix, New York, and San Francisco all add ten to twenty percent. Try renting from the hotel instead. Many large airports are close enough to cities where the same rental company does not charge surcharges and airport fees for the same car.

- Don't forget *you* are the customer. Often companies give you a car you don't like. It may be the model, the color, or that you wanted a two-door model and got a four door. You do not need to accept a car you don't like!

I flew into Los Angeles, collected my bags, and boarded a bus to the Hertz parking lot. Because I used Hertz frequently, I was dropped off at the express section. My name was up in lights directing me to stall 27. I arrived to find I had been given a Ford (I had specified a Toyota). Normally this would not have been a problem, but my meeting was with Toyota USA. For me to arrive in a competitor's car was, I reasoned, not a good idea. The Hertz representative informed me I could not request a specific car manufacturer. Her attitude was take it or leave it! I asked for the supervisor and got the same "we are very busy and you are not important" response. I reboarded the airport shuttle bus and returned to the airport. The first shuttle that came by was Budget. What a difference! At this location, they not only rent the standard compacts, mid-, and full-size cars, but exotic cars, as well.

*If half the rental car drivers disappeared from the 405 freeway right now, I'd be home already.*
— Harry Blackstone

Budget offered me a choice of a Rolls Royce, Ferrari, BMW, Mercedes, as well as a Toyota. I took a Toyota and made my meeting within ten minutes of my scheduled time. (Remember, if possible, to leave enough time to resolve these types of situations.) Now I only use Budget in L.A. if my timetable requires I pick up the car immediately from the airport and get on my way. For my personal choice, I use the franchise car rental in the hotel. I am often upgraded, certainly treated better, and often given an extra hour or so, at no charge, if I return the car later than expected. Remember, *you* are in the driver's seat.

*At a hotel, demand every convenience you rely on at home. Insist on getting your breakfast before your 6 A.M. jog, whether room service is open or not. There's no reason you shouldn't take advantage of people just because you're in a different town.*
— Molly Katz

## Chapter 23
# Renting a Room

When a friend of mine arrives at a hotel after a long trip, he flings open the door of his room and shouts, "Honey, I'm home!" He knows no one is in there to hear his greeting, but he also knows it makes him smile and, in some small way, helps him to adapt to his new home away from home.

The most important issue with a hotel is how you feel when you stay in the room for an extended period of time. At the same time, you must express how you want to feel to the various hotel staff members with whom you come in contact.

Sometimes when I travel — especially when I'm looking at the hotel as a potential sight for a group incentive program — I'm often upgraded to a larger room or a higher floor. In many instances, one of the amenities is a bathrobe. Those of you who travel know the size "One Size Fits All" is simply not true!

I am a large man. The normal robe found in hotels simply does not provide total coverage. In fact, a large part of me is left uncovered. The first time this happened, I called the front desk to request a larger size. I was told "One Size Fits All."

After many different ill-fitting robes and subsequent hotel visits and requests, I found the front desk or housekeeping staff had no options. Because I feel customer service is the benchmark of all companies providing goods or services, I decided I would make a point.

Once, after showering at a nice resort location, I put on the robe. I ordered room service and answered the door wearing the robe. As the server slammed the door and ran down the hall, I knew I should expect a call from management. "My robe doesn't fit," I told the manager. His answer? "One Size Fits All!" I explained I would continue to answer the door wearing my "One Size Fits All" bathrobe. In future visits, I found larger and smaller robes had been purchased by the resort. In some cases, they have even embroidered my name on it. They keep the robe at the property. When I arrive, it is laid out on the bed. Funny thing, though — the label still says "One Size Fits All."

Remember this is *your* home for as many days as you stay. Choose a hotel that offers you the best accommodations, safety, and amenities you require. I personally have found two chains in the U.S. that take care of my needs: Marriott and Hyatt. While others *could* do the job, I prefer to deal with as few hotels and, for that matter, airlines as possible. I would never fly Northwest, rent a specific car make or model from Hertz, or stay at a budget hotel. This does not mean these suppliers are going out of business because I don't use them. My preference is simply not to use them.

Once you determine what chain or specific hotel you want to stay at frequently, introduce yourself to the front desk manager.

# Chapter 23
## Dr. Travel Prescribes: Renting a Room

Tell him or her your projected number of visits, the duration of each visit, and your needs. For example, I go to L.A. every two weeks. I introduced myself to the director of sales at the LAX Hyatt (now owned by another hotel chain). I told the sales director I would like to rent a locker or space where I could keep my personal items, such as bathing suit, bath robe, slippers, dress shirt, and so forth. She said I should bring the items in a piece of luggage that locked and she would store it at no charge.

> *In a panic, a traveler called down to the hotel's front desk soon after checking in. 'Help!' he yelled. 'I'm trapped inside my room!'*
>
> *'What do you mean, trapped?'*
>
> *'Well, I see three doors,' the man explained. 'The first opens to a closet and the second opens to a bathroom. And the third door has a Do Not Disturb sign hanging on it!'*
>
> — Peter S. Greenberg

I also asked if I could reserve a specific room. While the hotel couldn't promise the room would always be unoccupied, it did have my room available about ninety-eight percent of the time. The increase in my productivity while I was living in L.A. was amazing!

## Hyatt Regency Fort Worth President Suite

Everything is bigger in Texas. After a long flight, which saw delays, substituted aircraft, and a replacement crew on one segment due to their flight time limits, I arrived in Forth Worth on my way from Boston. I called my friend Scott Walker at the Hyatt and explained I had an early morning meeting and needed a room. Unfortunately, all the hotels were totally sold out. With my after-midnight arrival, I was confident no rooms would be available. Scott told me to check my voice mail upon arrival.

I called in to find Scott's message indicating he was unable to solve my problem, but if I would go to the Hyatt Regency Fort

Part IV
Upon Arrival

Worth, they would try to find something. I reached the hotel at 2:45 A.M. My meeting was scheduled for 8:30 A.M. and it was thirty miles from the hotel. I was not happy, but I did not convey my displeasure to the front desk clerk.

When I presented my credit card for identification, the front desk clerk would not take it. He apologized and told me their computers were down. He also informed me that, because of numerous delays, no rooms were available. The desk clerk did receive a call from Scott, though, and he held a sleeping room, at no charge. I took the key and dragged myself to the elevator. Once I got off the elevator I realized the room was the last one at the end of a long, long hallway. Without the assistance of a bellman, I lugged the bag to the end of the hall. When I opened the door, I was amazed.

A large pair of long horn antlers hung over a leather bar in a room that must have been designed by Ernest Hemingway. Animal skins and leather made this the room with the most western theme outside of Mickey Gilley's. I was in the Presidential Suite! On the coffee table sat a note from Scott, apologizing because he could not find a roomier suite. Next to the card was an assortment of Texas beer, a large bottle of tequila, a bowl of blue corn chips, a gallon of salsa, and two pounds of guacamole. Just what I wanted at 3 A.M.!

I called the front desk. The clerk had anticipated my call. He responded: "Any problems, sir?" "Yes! I cannot eat or drink all this stuff. Can you send someone up to help?" I replied. Within ten minutes, security guards, housekeepers, kitchen staff, and even the front desk clerk arrived like locusts to join in the feeding frenzy. They left and sent in replacements, which lasted the remainder of the evening. That morning, while I got ready for the meeting, the phone rang. My meeting had been canceled. To disappoint me further, my conversation included a sobering announcement that the budget for the program had been eliminated entirely. No further conversation took place. All the delays, frustrations, and aggravations suddenly seemed unimportant. All I could remember was the fun time I spent in Fort Worth.

# Chapter 23
## Dr. Travel Prescribes: Renting a Room

At this moment, the bill for my room was slipped beneath the door. The amount? $1,954. On the copy were the signatures of everyone who had joined me that evening and a PAID stamp on the statement. I guess it's true . . . everything is bigger in Texas!

> *I stayed at a very exclusive hotel last week. Even room service had an unlisted number.*
> — George Burns

- If the hotel has a concierge desk, introduce yourself to the concierge. A concierge can arrange everything you may need, including transportation, theatre tickets, a tailor, restaurant suggestions, and reservations, interpreters, doctors, tour guides, and just about anything you think you need. If you are traveling on business to an unfamiliar city and want to continue with jogging or power walking, check with the concierge. Often he or she has maps of safe, scenic routes. Just remember to save some energy for the reason for your trip.

As a concierge for sixteen years in San Francisco, Holly Stiel told me the following story. "While helping three guests in front of me and keeping two guests on hold, a terribly unkempt person pushed his way to my desk and said in a loud voice 'Hey lady, I need a room for the night.'" Not wanting to upset her guests and knowing with certainty not to send the man to the front desk, Holly asked for clarification. He responded by telling her, "I have not slept in four days and I've got $3, so where are you going to send me?" Wanting to handle the situation with dignity, Holly took out a map (she even used a highlighter) and directed him to the closest shelter, telling him they would feed him there and put him up for the night. He left and she went about the business of helping her customers. A few days later, the same fellow returned to her desk and said, "Hey lady! Remember that shelter you sent me to?" Holly answered, "Of course." The man replied, "I didn't like it! What else you got?" *How perfect,* Holly thought, *only in San Francisco would the homeless use a concierge and then come back and complain!*

Tips are not expected, but they do go a long way to make your second request a priority. When they care enough to do the very best, a card simply will not do. I often give the concierge an autographed copy of my book, a **Shi<sup>f</sup>t Happens!**® pin, and some cash. In many cases, they have returned the cash, saying the book and pin were more than enough. Upon my return to that hotel, I am often asked for extra pins or books for their friends or business associates. And I have booked several speaking engagements through introductions by the concierge.

## ✈Travel Tip: Leisure versus Business

Always insist your weekend reservation be classified as *leisure*. If you say it is for business, there is a good chance the rate will be higher. If you cannot get a leisure rate, ask for the convention rate. You can normally get the reservation agent to offer it to you if you say you are going to the convention, which, technically you are, by staying at the convention hotel.

Other ways can make a hotel room more homelike. A few suggestions follow:

# Chapter 23
## Dr. Travel Prescribes: Renting a Room

## ✈Travel Tip: Keeping Comfort Up

- Take care of your back. If the desk or bureau is higher than the bed, pack or unpack your suitcase on it instead of the bed to avoid back strain.

- Ask for what you want. Ask housekeeping for such items as an extra pillow or two, a brighter light bulb, fresh towels, an iron, a hairdryer, and so forth. Or, ask the concierge for anything else, including information on restaurants, shopping, sites, walks, or jogging trails.

- What about noise? If noise in the hall or street keeps you awake, put the TV on to a nonbroadcasting channel, turn the brightness off, and let the gentle hissing sound (called *white noise*) cover outside noises and lull you to sleep.

> *Generally speaking, the length and grandness of a hotel's name are an exact opposite reflection of its quality. Thus, the Hotel Central will prove to be a clean, pleasant place in a good part of town and the Hotel Royal Majestic-Fantastic will be a fleabag next to a topless bowling alley.*
>
> — Miss Piggy

- Put away tent cards with advertising on them. Would you have ads all over your living room?

- If you use your computer and modem, make sure your room is modem-ready. Hotels and motels built before 1990 may not be equipped for computers. Also make sure your equipment needs are analog or digital. Plugging in the modem to the wrong line can cause a burn out of your computer's system.

- If you are a nonsmoker, request a nonsmoking room.

- Travel with sample sizes of your favorite bubble bath, mouthwash, or perfume. Familiar fragrances feel like home.

Part IV
Upon Arrival

- Newscaster-author Charles Kuralt advises "never sleep on the side of the bed next to the telephone." The side of the bed closest to the phone is destroyed because everyone else has slept on it. He also suggests traveling with safety pins to hold window curtains closed and a rubber stopper to keep the water in the sink.

- Get wet. Your hotel room, like the atmosphere of the plane you just left, is also a low-moisture environment. Windows often don't open and air is frequently recirculated. To counteract this, before you go to bed at night, fill the tub by running the shower and leave the bathroom door open. This does three things. First, it adds extra moisture to your room. Second, if a fire breaks out, you can quickly wet towels and put them under the hall door to prevent smoke from entering your room. Or, you can put wet towels over your head as you make your way out of the hotel. And, third, you can hang your travel-weary clothes in the steamy bathroom to get the wrinkles out.

DOCTOR TRAVEL FAMILY

- Decorate the room. Suzanne De Groot, a sales rep for a leading scarf manufacturer, uses her product samples to decorate

208

# Chapter 23
## Dr. Travel Prescribes: Renting a Room

her room. She changes an ordinary room into an extraordinary one. Move the furniture (those coffee tables are always in the way), get some flowers, or put family photos around.

- Wake-up calls. If you need to get up at a certain time, but you forgot your alarm clock, ask for two wake-up calls, ten to fifteen minutes apart.

- Before you go to sleep, check the clock radio in your room. The previous occupant may have had to get up at 4 A.M. and set the alarm accordingly. You may find yourself being awakened in the middle of the night by Conway Twitty.

*Hotel: A place where you trade dollars for quarters.*
— Steve Wilson

- Take along something to remind you of someone special. This helps to keep you connected, even though you are miles away. Edmund Boyle, a former traveling salesman, for example, tells about a stuffed penguin, complete with a note in its ear that reads "I Love My Dad!" given to him by Jeanine, his young daughter.

In *Guideposts* magazine, Boyle writes: "On my next trip, I tossed the penguin in my suitcase. That night when I called home, Jeanine was upset that the penguin had disappeared. 'Honey, he's here with me,' I explained, 'I brought him along.'

From then on, the penguin came with me — as essential as my briefcase or shaving kit. And we made friends along the way. In Albuquerque, I checked into a hotel, dumped out my bag, and dashed to a meeting. When I returned, the maid had turned down the bed and propped the penguin on the pillow. In Boston, I found it perched in a glass on the nightstand. Once a customs agent at New York's Kennedy Airport dug the penguin out of my suitcase and, holding it up, said, 'Thank God we don't charge a tax on love, or you'd owe a bundle.'

Part IV
Upon Arrival

One night I discovered the penguin was missing and, after a frantic phone call, I learned I'd left it in my previous hotel room, where it had been rescued by a maid. I drove a hundred miles to retrieve it and when I arrived at midnight, the penguin was waiting at the front desk. Jeanine is in college now, and I don't travel as much. The penguin sits on my dresser, a reminder that love is a wonderful traveling companion. All those years on the road, it was the one thing I never left home without."

- How do hotels determine which room to assign you? Unlike airline seats, most hotel guests are indifferent about guestrooms. Without any request for a preference, the rooms are assigned randomly. Rooms are clustered so housekeepers can clean the rooms more efficiently. In addition, the concept of several people on a floor adds a level of security, which is lost when you find yourself alone on a floor. Should this happen (this is *highly* unlikely), ask to be moved.

Hotels, like airlines, are finding the benefits of frequent stayers. Enroll in every frequency program you can find. In this way, you can flash all your cards at check-in and the front desk clerk will react as if you were one of his hotel's better guests. The clerk sees the high level of competition and wants to make a favorable impression. Remember, if you don't ask, you will most likely not receive. Just like airlines, hotels do have upgrades available at the discretion of the front line personnel. But be fair to them, as well. (I have a friend who is a chain smoker, who does not want to stay in rooms for smokers because they smell. I always make him stay in a smoking room out of fairness to others. We don't travel together often any more.)

## ✈Travel Tip: Keeping Costs Down

- Save money before you get to the hotel. Many hotels have courtesy transportation to and from the airport. Instead of paying the exorbitant taxi fare, call the hotel on their free 800 number or from the display board near the luggage carousels at the airport.

# Chapter 23
## Dr. Travel Prescribes: Renting a Room

- Never use the dry cleaning or laundry service from the hotel. A recent survey by Corporate Travel found these prices at five hotels that were called randomly: suit: $12.77; dress: $10.48; bra: $2.81; shirt: $3.80; socks: $1.77; underwear: $2.46.

Look up a cleaner in the Yellow Pages. In many cases, cleaners will pick up and deliver to the hotel for less than the hotel charges.

> *What bed and breakfast jargon really means:*
> *Antiques: Beaten-up furniture*
> *Casual: Make your own bed*
> *Cozy: Your room has less square footage than your suitcase*
> *Romantic: No electricity — candles required*
> *Rustic: The plumbing is out back*
> — *Rocky Mountain News*

- Many restaurants and fast food places deliver to hotels. Rather than pay the hotel for a ten-inch pizza, call a restaurant and order the family special, including a soft drink for less, including the tip.

Part IV
Upon Arrival

- Ask for a room with a refrigerator. You can also empty the minibar (before you do, make certain the minibar is not tied to the computer for automatic billing). Then place leftovers or other foods you purchase outside the hotel inside the mini bar.

- Boil food, or cook it, or peel it to avoid traveler's diarrhea. Even fruit whose skin is normally eaten, like apples, should be peeled when traveling, says Allison Clough, M.D., M.P.H., Travel and Geographic Medicine Clinic, Tucson, Arizona.

- Location, location, location! Just as in airline fares, hotels charge a wide range of rates for a room — depending on such factors as time of year, day of the week, how much business they have, the location of your room, and more.

*Location:* Downtown hotels are often higher priced than facilities further away or near the airport.

*Room without a view:* Resort hotels typically charge more for a room with a view of the ocean or mountains than for a room that looks upon a garden or valley. Determine how much a view is worth to you before you make your reservations.

*Season:* Off-season rates drop dramatically. For the best rates, check out the summer in the Sun Belt or the winter in northern non-ski resorts.

*Day of week/nonresort versus resort:* In most hotels, discounted rates are offered for the weekend (Friday, Saturday, and Sunday). But at resort properties, no discount is offered for the weekend. In fact, in many instances, the price increases. If you can be flexible, ask for the best rate at any time of the year. Also ask which days of the week are reduced.

An empty hotel room is inventory that cannot be sold the next day. Hotels track occupancy. If you approach a hotel when they need *bodies* to stay in them, the rates normally quoted are totally negotiable. Don't forget to ask! Or . . .

# Chapter 23
## Dr. Travel Prescribes: Renting a Room

- Haggle! To obtain the best hotel room rate, negotiate over the telephone before you get there, not while you're standing at the front desk. And negotiate with the reservation manager, not with a desk clerk, who may not have the authority to wheel and deal. Often you can get the best deal on the same day you need a room because, if it isn't booked that night, it won't bring in any money. If you don't like the first offer, call back later and try again. Ask the person with whom you're speaking when the shift changes and make your call just as the shift is leaving. In an effort to get home, they may give you a better deal simply to get you off the phone.

> *Nothing is more perishable than tonight's unreserved hotel room.*
> — Gerald Michaelson

Most of us, though, can't wait until the day of our arrival to book a room. So Burt Dubin, of the Personal Achievement Institute in Kingman, Arizona, came up with an absolutely, positively, sure-fire way to get the lowest hotel rate. First, Dubin advises, call the 800 number and ask for the rate for the dates you want. Then ask for the corporate rate for those same dates. Then ask what seasonal specials they have. If you're planning to stay over a weekend, ask what weekend packages the hotel has. Then ask, "Is that your lowest rate?" After they respond, ask what their supersaver rate is. Then say "Thanks" and hang up.

Next call the hotel directly and ask the same questions. Then pick the best deal and book your room. And remember to guarantee your reservation with a credit card, to get a confirmation number, and to write down the name of the person who agreed to the deal!

The Doral Hotel in Miami Beach, Florida, is considered by many to be the preeminent address to stay at while in Miami. Christopher Perks, vice president/general manager, asked me to evaluate his plans for a new Presidential Suite, designed for presidents, kings, other heads of state, rock musicians, well-heeled business men, or anyone who could pay the tariff or the hotel wanted to upgrade.

The suite was actually two suites — an east and a west wing. Each suite had two bedrooms with four bathrooms. A formal dining room adjoined a large sitting area that housed three TVs, stacked one on top of another, and one larger TV to the left of the stack, for a total of four television sets. The purpose was to enable the guest to watch and listen to the big screen while watching, but not listening to, the others. In this way, the guest could have CNN on the big screen and the major networks on the other three sets. A full kitchen, butler service, private chef, and a hot tub on the deck overlooking Miami Beach and the city made this the perfect recluse. Even the elevator required a separate pass key and security code to gain admission (this was changed after each guest checked out of the suite).

Because the suites were not yet completed, my walk-through was an attempt to visualize completion and make suggestions or alterations. Room after room was perfection. It was well-thought out, professionally executed, and user friendly.

When I reached the bathroom, I discovered a missing element. No heated towel rack. In Europe, many hotels are still heated by steam. Hot water pipes run through the bathroom and towels are hung on them. This heats the towel. One of life's little pleasures is a hot towel on a cold morning. Yet here, within the confines of Nirvana, none was to be found. I suggested to Christopher that a heated towel rack be added to each bathroom, to which he immediately agreed. This seemed a fitting suggestion to complete the total experience of staying in the suite.

About a month later, I received a Doral towel with a note that read: "Warm it yourself. Your idea cost us $10,000 to comply with electrical requirements, safety regulations, the fire department, and so forth. Next time keep your idea and this towel."

- Hotel alternatives. When we travel, most of us think of

# Chapter 23
## Dr. Travel Prescribes: Renting a Room

spending the night in a hotel or a motel. But other, sometimes less expensive, more attractive, places exist to stay.

*Bed and breakfasts* (B&Bs) may not always offer the amenities of hotels (like a swimming pool or round-the-clock room service), but they are friendlier and frequently make up for these deficiencies with charm and a more personal touch.

*Back to school:* For summer travel, 700 university residence halls are open to the public. Many have park-like settings and offer tennis, swimming, museums, and more.

> *The net worth of the average minibar slightly exceeds that of the people who use it.*
> — Bob Baseman

*Youth hostels:* These may have mostly bunk-style beds, but frequently they also have a private couples or family room if you request it well in advance. In addition, some are situated in quaint buildings, such as the one in California housed in an old lighthouse.

- Reach out and gouge someone. Before you make a mountain of phone calls, find out the hotel rates. Some hotels charge as much as $1 for local calls, connecting to an 800 number or for a number from information. The same calls would be a fraction of the cost (or free) in the lobby. If you do call from your room and you are going to be making several calls, press the # symbol after the first person hangs up, and then dial the next number. This will save another hotel charge to connect you to your long-distance carrier.

- Beware of the minibar in your room. Those goodies can usually be found less expensively in the lobby gift shop and for even less at the corner grocery. To avoid an issue at checkout, I suggest you do not accept the minibar key. Ask the front desk to make a note on your folio. This way, you won't be charged for anything in the minibar. Also be careful! Many minibars place items on top of the minibar. These items look like they are free gifts from the hotel. Even the most experienced traveler has been caught opening a jar of macadamia nuts from a jar with the logo of the hotel printed on it, while thinking this is a welcome gift from the general manager.

How do hotels decide what to put in the minibars? And why is everything in the minibars so expensive? When hotel management sees something selling briskly in their lounges, restaurants, or coffee shops, they stock it in the minibar. They know many of us are too lazy to get dressed and walk down the hall, to the elevator, or to the shop when what we want is right next to the bed. And, because each minibar can cost up to $1,800, that's a lot of sodas, peanuts, and cheese to sell!

- Reduced room rates

*Discounters:* Just like airline consolidators, hotel discounters contract with various lodgings to buy blocks of rooms that may otherwise go empty. They then pass part of the volume discount on to you. The drawback? Most are only available in major cities and only at a limited number of hotels.

*Corporate rates:* Ask for the corporate rate. Many hotels will give you the corporate rate even if you are not associated with a company. Be aware, though, you may do better with some of the other discounts listed in this section.

*Senior-student discounts:* Even if you are not an AARP (American Association of Retired Persons) member, but you're over age 55, ask for a senior discount. Students, too, get discounts. And you don't have to be under age 25. Schools that offer continuing education courses frequently issue student ID cards even if you are taking only one class.

*Government discounts:* Ask for the government rate if you are in the military or work for a government agency.

*Membership discounts:* Being a member of a major organization,

# Chapter 23
## Dr. Travel Prescribes: Renting a Room

like AAA or AARP, may get you the best discount of all. I discovered an AARP card gives a higher discount than the government rate.

> *As my good friend Al Capp told me a few years ago, the best thing to do with a confirmed [hotel] reservation slip when you have no room is to spread it out on the sidewalk in front of the hotel and go to sleep on it. You'll either embarrass the hotel into giving you a room or you'll be hauled off to the local jug, where at least you'll have a roof over your head.*
> — Art Buchwald

*Promotional-weekend packages:* Check your daily and Sunday newspapers for special hotel deals. Some have a special weekend package deal to entice you to fill up the rooms vacated by business folks who stay only on weekdays. Promotions can include such amenities as free breakfast, golf, or tennis.

*Discount travel club:* These clubs offer savings on major chain hotels of up to 50 percent for any night of the week. Join one!

*Convention rate:* If you are attending a meeting at the hotel, ask if they have a reduced rate for attendees.

- *Long-term stay rates:* Ask if you can get a discount if you plan to stay more than five consecutive nights or if you plan to come back often. I stayed at one hotel twenty-three times in one year, for two nights each visit. The hotel reduced its rate to me more than fifty percent and upgraded me to a suite whenever possible. That the hotel is part of a big chain is unimportant. Hotels are still operated by people who believe in keeping customers happy. You may get a discounted rate because you have attained *preferred* status in the hotel's frequent stayer program, but you get *personal* treatment because you got up close and personal.

- *Overbooking:* Like the airlines, hotels also overbook. You cannot be 100 percent certain the hotel won't give away your room before you arrive, but you can minimize the chance of this happening by guaranteeing your reservation with a check or credit card and by getting a confirmation receipt.

If you plan to arrive after 6 P.M. call the hotel and tell the front desk you are on your way. Also, if you need to cancel your credit card confirmed reservation, make sure you do so by 6 P.M. or you'll be billed for a night's lodging.

If you do have a guaranteed reservation backed by a credit card and the hotel still gives away your room, ask for an upgrade or a transfer to a comparable hotel. Do not think hotels are governed by the same rules as the airlines. There is no FAA equivalent for hotels. Thousands of owners exist instead of a few. Most hotels are not publicly traded.

Here's a story to show you even the busiest resort hotels find time and compassion for their customers. The winner of a trip to Hawaii called me from her airport in Indianapolis. She was sure we had not sent her airline tickets, even though the winner announcement letter had been received by her husband more than two months before the trip. She had checked her luggage with the skycap and proceeded to the gate to check in. After searching through her purse, her husband's briefcase, and all other carry-on belongings, she called our office to complain. With her connecting flight leaving in less than fifteen minutes, we researched our files to find the tickets were shipped in the same package as the winner's letter. Because the express package had been signed for by her husband, I asked to speak to him.

> *Why stay at better hotels? Because they can do laundry in a few hours. Because they have room service when it's 3 A.M., but your body thinks it's dinnertime. Because they know places you don't. Because they sew buttons, press faster, have clout with maitre d's, offer feather pillows, have the electrical adapter you forgot, feed your dog, and remember your name.*
> — Hal Rubensten and Jim Mullen

# Chapter 23
## Dr. Travel Prescribes: Renting a Room

"When you received the letter?" I asked. "Do you remember anything else about the day? Was it cold? Raining? Did you get the letter prior to going to work or after?" After a few questions, the man remembered he had just come back from picking up his new leather coat. He was so excited about getting the letter, he had placed the tickets inside the coat. When he went inside the house, he hung the coat in the closet where it remained until this day.

Because the plane was leaving, we had no choice but to ask the airport to get their bags and reschedule them for a later flight while they drove home to get the tickets. After getting their car from the parking lot, driving 158 miles round trip, the couple arrived at the airport in time to catch the last flight to Chicago. Weather delays caused the cancellation of the last flight. The couple had to stay overnight in Chicago. And because many airlines do not pay for weather-caused delays, the couple had to pay for their own room.

Meanwhile, we called the resort to advise them the couple missed their flight. The resort agreed to hold the room, but charged us for the late cancellation. Upon arrival in Honolulu, the couple tried to check into the hotel without credit cards. They had never traveled before, so they didn't know cash was unacceptable as a credit reference (funny how money is no longer representative of credit worthiness).

The front desk clerk could not violate the check-in policy, so the couple was denied a room. They called our office again. This time, I called the general manager of the hotel and explained the situation. He offered to check in the winners if they presented a deposit of $500. About thirty minutes later, I received a call from the winners to learn they had only taken $400 with them for the seven-day trip. And they had already spent $150 on the room rental, dinner, and parking. They simply did not bring enough cash for this kind of trip. Most important, their trip, the prize they had won, did not include meals.

The general manager and I discussed the situation. He informed me these two winners looked and acted like something from *The*

*Real McCoys* television series. They had never traveled, had never been outside their immediate farming community, and did not understand the protocol of flying to a posh Hawaiian resort, paying for meals, or needing credit cards. The general manager was moved by their honesty and lack of pretense, however, and he was genuinely sympathetic toward the situation.

Between the generosity of both the general manager and our company, we provided the couple's meals, took care of all their activities, and even upgraded them to a concierge floor in the hotel, so they could have access to the breakfast and early evening complimentary meal services. I notified the sponsor of the trip, who provided an additional $1,000 in spending money to cover souvenirs, a 35mm camera, and some "happy" shirts. We all wanted this trip to be a once-in-a-lifetime experience and it was for all of us.

## ✈Travel Tip: Special Combination Offers

- Many hotels and airlines get together to offer special rates to their frequent flyer members. Always ask about special combination offers. Do not accept the first price offered. Period! Check your frequent flyer newsletters. Each month the airlines, hotels, and car rentals offer special rates at selected hotels.

> *What a hotel: The towels were so big and fluffy, you could hardly close your suitcase.*
> — Henny Youngman

> *In my hotel, you push a button and you can go to any state or planet you want. It is supposed to be "Worlds of Fun," and whatever you want comes right to you.*
> — Haley Pearson, fourth grade

## ✈Travel Tip: Check-In and Check-Out Times

- Why does housekeeping come to the room at 9 A.M., but when I check-in at 3 P.M., my room isn't ready? Housekeepers often check with the front desk to learn which guests have requested early wakeup calls. Early wakeup calls often result in early check-outs. Many guests do not check out at the requested hotel check-out time, though. Often guests request a late check-out, especially those with Diamond status (Hyatt's program) or Platinum level (Marriott's program). Both of these programs are the equivalent of frequent flyer programs, where points are awarded for staying at the hotel. In some cases, the hotel will extend a later check-out time because of this preferred status.

## ✈Travel Tip: Early Departure Penalties

- Check-out penalties. Early departure penalties may be a problem if you are booking a hotel for more than one night. Most charge only for the nights you actually stay, but some charge a penalty for early check-out. Make sure you understand the rules. If you change your plans often, avoid hotels or chains that charge penalties. Or, discuss your needs with the front desk manager. Management may be willing to make an exception in the hope you'll return again.

## ✈Travel Tip: Broadway Plays

When you are looking for house seats to Broadway shows, call the Actor's Fund of America and ask for Fund Tix (212-221-7300). The tickets are double the price, but half goes to charity and the seats are great. For a brief description of Broadway shows, call 212-563-2929.

## ✈Travel Tip: Keeping Safe

- Switch rooms if the front desk blares out your room number.

- Make sure your phone works.

- Avoid walking down long hallways — ask for a room near the elevator or the stairs.

Part IV
Upon Arrival

- Keep a light on in your room when you go out. If it's not on when you return, don't enter.

- When you're in your room, don't open the door unless you know for certain who is on the other side.

- Ask the hotel to lock your valuables in a safe deposit box (and get a written receipt for what's in it). If something is stolen from your room, state laws limit the hotel's responsibility from a mere $50 to about $500.

- Always leave your hotel room key in the same place — so you can find it quickly in an emergency.

> *This towel bar was once very happy, because a family of soft, cushy towels once lived there. Sadly, they've all been kidnapped and taken to faraway places, never to be together at home again. Please do not break up this family, they're at home, where they belong. If you find it absolutely necessary to take a member of our family with you, they're available for adoption at the front desk for a moderate price.*
> — Seen by Jeff Blackman, J.D., C.S.P., near a towel bar in a Radisson Hotel

- Some lodgings are built on the fringes of not-so-great areas. Before you go for a walk, ask the front desk or guest services for a map and suggested routes.

- Know where the fire alarm is on your floor.

- If the fire alarm goes off, grab your key before you leave your room. This way, you can get back in when all is clear.

- Before you unpack, locate the nearest fire exit from your room. Count the number of doors you pass to get there.

- In case of fire, you may be better off staying in your room. If so, wet some towels and place them on the floor near the door to prevent smoke from entering your room.

# Chapter 23
## Dr. Travel Prescribes: Renting a Room

- If there is a fire and you must evacuate, take the stairs, not the elevator. Don't open your door if it is hot to touch. Crawl low under the smoke.

- If fire is a major concern to you, always ask for a room on the lower floors. It is easier to get out, fire hoses can reach your room, and a ladder may also be available.

- If the room has an ironing board, use it to hold the door closed by putting the ironing board against the door, under the lock, door handle, or other secure part of the door to brace it from being opened from the outside. Remember, others may have keys in their possession. Only electronic locks provide new key codes for each stay.

- Hotels are run by people for people. This isn't brain surgery. You want a clean, comfortable room at a fair price. Simple enough?

## ✈Travel Tip: Becoming a Hotel VIP

You needn't be a VIP to get VIP service. The key is to tip early and often. Offer the doorman, bellhop, and maid $5–$20 the first time you see them. Provide the tip whether or not you need extra

## Part IV
### Upon Arrival

service. Make sure the manager and concierge know your name (give them your business card). If your product isn't too costly, offer them a sample. Treat them as if they were your customers. Contrive some reason to consult them (dinner suggestions, running track, shopping tips, and so forth). Tip for each and every opportunity. Remember to make them feel important and they will make you feel like a VIP.

I was in Las Vegas for COMDEX, one of the largest trade exhibits for computers, software, and such. When I checked into Caesar's, I tipped the bell man $20. I told him I would need some room service and I wanted him to select the best server. By the time I got to my room, room service was on the phone and offered to come to my room to discuss my needs.

I told the server I would be entertaining all week and wanted to keep an open bar, dry snacks, fruits, and cheeses in the room. I wanted the room consumption to be monitored by room service because maids normally don't provide room service assistance. Because I had rented a mini-suite, there was a formal area with a bar and refrigerator.

> *Go to the bar in any hotel in the late afternoon. Dozens of business travelers are talking about how tough their jobs are, the troubles in their marriage, how miserable their kids are, how the crime rate is soaring and no one's doing anything about it, and how poorly Congress runs the country. So why is it called "Happy Hour"?*
> — Gracie Fields

The agreed-upon charge for the first set up was $150. I tipped the server $50. He was thrilled. Remember, I was in Vegas and lots of big tippers are there.

The first day, I had only one meeting and served a few bottles of soft drinks and a little fruit. The second day, the meetings were not held in the hotel. The third day, I had to spend the entire day on

### Chapter 23
### Dr. Travel Prescribes: Renting a Room

the tradeshow floor to get more evening appointments. So for three days no meetings were held in my room. I had spent $150 for a few pieces of fruit and soft drinks . . . not a great bargain. And now, most of the food had to be replaced.

I called my server and told him I would have about four dozen people in my room over the next six hours. I asked him to replace the fruit and cheese and to bring some hot appetizers. The first meeting was at 5:30 P.M. My schedule indicated I would have the heaviest attendance from 8:30 to 10:30 P.M.

Shortly before the first meeting, the server arrived with exactly what I'd ordered. He asked about the function, the number of guests, and the reason for the meetings. He seemed interested in my business. I gave him another $20 and told him to check back each hour.

Half an hour later the first guest arrived. After my presentation, I was told the guests were going to dinner. They had a drink and left. The second presentation involved six people who had a few appetizers and a drink. An hour later, about four dozen people arrived. At the same time, the server stopped by to check on the food. He saw the crowd and told me he'd return momentarily.

Within fifteen minutes, the server arrived with a dazzling display of crab claws, shrimp, and lobster, plus sushi, sashimi, cooked scallops, mussels, corn on the cob, and vegetables. One of the larger computer companies had had a reception — a Cape Cod Lobster Bake — that had ended at 6:30 P.M. The server and the bell man went to the room, captured the display, condensed it onto a serving cart, and delivered it to my room. My guests were impressed with the food and what they perceived as my being a spectacular host. "No charge!" the server whispered. "You have been nice to us and we want to replay you for your kindness."

To understand the hotel industry more fully and to get the most out of your stay, write to:

Part IV
Upon Arrival

American Society of Travel Agents
1101 King Street
Alexandria, Virginia 22314

Include a self-addressed, business-size envelope. The brochure on the hotel industry includes an explanation of common hotel and resort terms. And it's free.

*Food is an important part of a balanced diet.*
— Fran Lebowitz

## Chapter 24
# Son of Travel Broadens

If maintaining a healthy diet at home is difficult, maintaining one on the road is nearly impossible. Once I presented a program in a meeting room adjacent to a remote picnic area. Because the meeting was held in the south, typical southern food was served: fried catfish, fried hush puppies, and french-fried potatoes. The only fresh vegetable was a small container of coleslaw swimming in mayonnaise.

This southern fare was far from the low-fat diet I try to follow and I was far from any restaurant. Unless I wanted to fast that evening, I had no choice but to eat fried food. Although everything tasted good, this experience showed me eating healthy food on the road isn't always easy.

Sometimes eating on the road means dining in unfamiliar surroundings, at odd hours, on overcooked food, and with limited choices. For this reason I take breakfast bars, granola bars, dried fruit, and other easy to pack foods that don't require refrigeration. I hope the road food tips in this chapter help you improve those less-than-ideal meals and expand your choices.

## ✈Travel Tip: Finding Good Eats

- Ask the front desk or concierge at your hotel.

- Ask shopkeepers where they eat (not which restaurants they recommend).

- Inexpensive vegetarian restaurants can often be found near college campuses.

- If a restaurant looks interesting, but you are not sure how good it will be, wait outside and ask those who are leaving about the meal.

- Check my Web site at http://www.doctor-travel.com.

## ✈Travel Tip: Make Meals Memorable

- Go for interesting grub. Look for local specialties or ethnic foods you may not get at home.

- For a change of pace, order from room service if you always eat in restaurants. Do the same when you anticipate long lines at the hotel's restaurant or when you need to eat and run.

> *I went to a restaurant. It said, 'Breakfast anytime.' So I ordered French toast during the Renaissance.*
> — Steven Wright

- Introduce yourself to the owner or chef. In many cases, he or she will prepare a special meal for you or attempt to make you feel at home in another way. Try this! You may be amazed. Frequently the food bill is not presented at all. While this certainly isn't my main reason for introducing myself, it's a nice benefit. Of course, I always leave the owner or chef with an ATTITUDE or **Shift Happens!**® pin.

## ✈Travel Tip: Feast for Less

- Eat your main meal at lunch when prices are lower.
- Look for the reduced prices of the "Early Bird Special."
- Stay at hotels that offer complimentary breakfast or hors d'oeuvres.
- Select food from a nearby grocery or supermarket and have a picnic in the park or in your room.
- Join the frequent stayer programs for each hotel chain where you stay more than twice a year. Your monthly statements often contain upgrades and special offers for dining in the hotel.
- Upgrade to the concierge level or club level. Breakfast hors d'oeuvres and late night snacks are part of each of the amenities. Some club levels, like the Ritz Carlton, offer up to five food presentations throughout the day.

My personal favorite club levels are at the Hyatt Cypress Gardens (Orlando), the New York Marriott Marquis (Times Square), the Grand Hyatt Hong Kong, the Ritz Carlton Kapalua (Maui), and the Grand Hyatt Singapore.

## ✈Travel Tip: Eat Healthy

- Forget the entree. Instead, order a meal of appetizers, soup, plain baked potato, or salad.

- Ask for salad dressings or rich sauces on the side. Dip your fork into it, rather than pouring it over everything.

- Tell the waitperson to leave the butter in the kitchen.

- Ask for an egg substitute instead of real eggs.

- Ask how foods are prepared. Opt for broiled, baked, or steamed over fried, creamed, or buttered. As Dr. Roy Vartabedian says, "the more fried foods you eat, the sooner you die." Dr. Vartabedian's book, *Nutripoints*, explains how to eat foods in certain orders so they work to burn off calories without worrying about fats, sugar, and sodium. With his system, there is no cholesterol counting.

> *Health food makes me sick.*
> — Calvin Trillin

- Order from the fitness sections of restaurant menus. Sometimes they're listed as "Heart healthy meals" or "Spa cuisine."

- Don't clean your plate. When I was growing up, I had to eat everything on my plate. It was after World War II and I was told over and over again, "children are starving in Europe." Once I recall passing my plate, which still contained uneaten food, to my mother and saying, "Maybe you could send this to them." I learned then "time out" was not only available in sports. Since then, I learned I needn't eat everything on my plate, even if I like the meal. This has proven useful when I'm watching what and how much I eat during a trip.

- Split orders with your dining partner.

- Skip dessert. If you can't, order one and share!

- Eat breakfast. If you don't, you'll probably snack more throughout the day.

# Chapter 24
## Dr. Travel Prescribes: Son of Travel Broadens

- Beware of muffins. Muffins can contain more fat than doughnuts. If you must have a muffin, only eat the top.

- Avoid buffets. The food sits for long periods of time and it's tempting to overeat. If you do go to a buffet, scan the entire display of food before making your selections, take small portions, and fill your plate only once.

- To supplement what you eat, consider taking a multivitamin or an antioxidant (which contain Vitamins A, C, and E). You can also carry a meal replacement supplement for those times when having a real meal is impossible.

- Avoid fats and excess sugar. Fat dulls your mind and enhances fatigue. Sugars give you an initial burst of energy, but then make you tired.

- At airports, seek out restaurants and snack bars that serve such healthy foods as fresh fruit cups, bagels with fat-free cream cheese, nonsalted pretzels, dried fruits, nonfat yogurt, and so forth. Also, if time permits, eat at the international terminal. Often you'll find an Asian restaurant where you can get some stir-fried vegetables and rice.

- Choose lightly cooked vegetables over salads. Sometimes salads leave you feeling unsatisfied, with a tendency to want sugar snacks later.

- Eat protein for power, carbohydrates for calm. When you want to stay awake, eat high protein meals such as poached or broiled fish, or chicken. When you want to go to bed or be mellow, eat carbohydrates such as pasta, rice, pancakes, or bread.

- Do whatever it takes to eat wisely. Nutrition counselor, Annette Globits, for example, has her clients remember this rhyme: "When having breakfast at your favorite deli, say, 'Hold the butter and pass the jelly (sugar free).'"

> *I will not eat oysters. I want my food dead — not sick, not wounded — dead.*
> — Woody Allen

- Take your own food. Instant oatmeal or freeze-dried soups, for example, make a quick, light meal if you travel with your own heating coil for hot water. Take dried fruits, granola bars, breakfast bars, and nonfat candies. Some are exceptionally good.
- I like the following products.

Health Valley (1-800-423-4846) Healthy Tarts. They are fat free, have no cholesterol, and are fairly low in sugar. Calories per tart total 150. I have also found eating fresh fruit throughout the day provides me with sustained energy.

Quaker Chewy Granola Bars (available in most grocery stores). These come in several flavors. I like the variety pack, which offers several choices. Some are very low in fat, while others are not.

Slim Fast Nutritional Snack Bars (available in most grocery stores) come in several flavors. These are low in fat and sugar, but each flavor balances fat with sugar. Just like most foods, the snack bars are a great substitute for regular candy bars. They are not really low calorie, though, unless you compare them to regular candy bars.

Trader Joe's dried fruits in various mixtures. If you are ever in California, find a Trader Joe's. This is, without a doubt, one of the best sources for dried fruits and nuts anywhere. Trader Joe's labels are easy to read and the food products are exceptional. Call 1-800-746-7857 to find one of their locations. This chain also recently opened on the East Coast.

My suggestion is you carry some of these products with you when you travel. Sometimes delays or your ultimate location prevent you from eating a meal at your normal time. On one flight, we sat on the tarmac for over five hours. The flight had a 4:30 P.M. scheduled departure. No food, including peanuts, were served. We were constantly informed of our imminent take-off, but weather issues prevented departure time after time. My seatmates were grateful to me for providing something — anything — to eat during the delay. One grateful passenger gave me his business card and said to call him and he would take me to dinner the next time. As it turned out, we share an interest in wine and he became one of my most important clients. Remember, you are what you eat, or with whom you eat!

Part IV
Upon Arrival

*Mr. Universe: Don't forget, Mr. Carson, your body is the only home you'll ever have.*

*Johnny Carson: Yes, my home is pretty messy. But I have a woman who comes in once a week.*
*— The Tonight Show*

# Chapter 25
# Staying in Shape When You're Out of Town

Keeping fit on the road not only includes healthy eating; it also includes exercise. Here are a few low-key, high-return suggestions.

## Travel Secret: I-Hate-to-Exercise Exercises

- Instead of taking the elevator, climb the stairs to your room. For every five stairs you climb, you burn one calorie.

- Get out of your hotel and walk. You get exercise and you get to know your surroundings. And you don't need any special equipment. With only a pair of comfortable shoes, you can get all the exercise you need. Shopping malls and museums are safe places for solo walkers, but don't wear fanny packs (they're too easy to unfasten) and don't use backpacks (they can be cut from behind).

- Schedule an outdoor walking meeting instead of a meeting in a stuffy conference room.

- Check your hotel's exercise facilities. Many hotels have swimming pools, aerobic centers, jogging paths, and some even

Part IV
Upon Arrival

have closed-circuit exercise videos. Remember to pack appropriate clothing for these activities.

- Take your own workout audio cassette and player for a workout in the privacy of your room.

- Pack and use a jump rope or inflatable weights you can fill with water.

- Do a few sit-ups or push-ups while you watch the morning news.

- Take some exercise rubber bands. They weigh little and can be both aerobic and isometric.

- Check the local television guide for follow-along aerobic or yoga programs.

My favorite story about exercising took place in the Black Forest. Several of my colleagues were in Germany for a seminar and decided to spend an extra day or two sightseeing. On the first morning, we were all exhausted. We had a full day of seminars, drove over 150 miles to an inn, and had a very late, very cold dinner.

As the sun came through my window the following morning, I heard the strange sound of stones being crushed. I looked out the window to find my friend, a born-again health nut of recent months, running around in a circle on the stone driveway. He was dodging in between cars and horse-drawn carriages in somewhat of a homemade obstacle course.

And he was running with hand weights. Two of them — I could not believe it! Here was an experienced traveler, carrying thirty pounds of extra weight in his suitcases. He paid the airline for this privilege. He had to over tip the bell man, who could barely carry the bags up the stairs of the inn. When I shouted to him, "Why not take weights you can fill with water and then empty them until the next stop?" He stopped, looked at me in disbelief, and said, "They make them empty?"

> *I get exercise acting as a pallbearer to my friends who exercised.*
> — Chauncey Depew

# Chapter 26
# Cruise Control for Auto-Pilots

Cruise ships are actually floating hotel rooms. The enchantment starts as soon as your luggage arrives, the ship disembarks, and you are underway. Cruise ships are the same as the all-inclusive hotel or resort except they float. They also move. Champagne, fresh flowers, at least five meals a day, casinos, spas, pools, and gyms all add to the list of amenities included on most large cruise ships.

To many, a moving hotel room is disturbing. To others, the mere mention of a cruise makes their palms sweat, fingers twitch, and toes tap. Today's cruise ships are super liners that carry over 2,000 passengers to exotic ports of call or kill time by making large circles in the Atlantic and Pacific Ocean.

First let's set the record straight. Less than ten percent of all flyers have taken a cruise. Second, cruise lines enjoy a fairly high percent of repeat passengers. Third, no matter what you like to do, eat, or drink, a cruise line exists that exceeds your expectations. Fourth, no matter who you are or when you travel, you will have a definite opinion about cruising. Taking a cruise is not a passive event. Most women like cruises, while men are less prone to take the plunge.

Today's cruise companies are conglomerates that offer merchandise, tours, souvenir photographs, imprinted paraphernalia, liquor, cigarettes, cigars, watches, entertainment, gambling, Broadway-type shows, bingo, off-boat tours, and more. These ships travel to every exotic and glamorous ports of call: Italy, Hawaii, Grand Cayman, Catalina, Cozumel, Puerto Rico, the Panama Canal, and Alaska. Tour packages complete the experience by providing everything from submarine trips, horseback riding, mountain climbing, golf, tennis, and more.

Unlike any other form of travel accommodation, the cruise experience is an all-inclusive package, which can include airfare, transfers, all meals, all entertainment, dancing, aerobics, swimming pools, game rooms, and so forth. The packaging of components for cruise companies may include specific functions for golfers, wine enthusiasts, motivational speakers, training, and other forms of education. You should fully understand what is, and what is not, included in the cost of the ticket. Make sure you inquire about port charges, federal taxes, fees, and mandatory gratuities. A cruise is an all-inclusive vacation.

## ✈Travel Tip: Muddied Waters Can Be Cleared

Make sure you fully understand all the charges included in the cruise price. Read the fine print. Get comparable costs from other cruise lines that travel the same route. Until the government understands that add-on charges may not be passed along to the port authority or other regulatory agencies, please ask questions.

# Chapter 26
## Dr. Travel Prescribes: Cruise Control... for Auto Pilots

*If we don't change direction soon, we'll end up where we're going.*
— Professor Irwin Corey

A list of major cruise lines is provided, but this industry, while expanding in scope, is quickly becoming consolidated among several large companies. For instance, Carnival Cruise Lines, once called "The K Mart of the Caribbean," has had the last laugh. Carnival now controls the marketplace. It is, without a doubt, one of the best marketers and promoters of cruising. Carnival now owns more ships, other cruise lines, and support facilities than any one cruise company in the world. With acquisitions of Holland America, Costa Cruises, and Windstar Sailing Ships, Carnival's family can provide an introductory cruise for the neophyte or a trip to the Mediterranean, Russia, Hawaii, or Alaska for the more sophisticated traveler.

Susan Joseph, of Carnival Cruise Lines, tells the story of a man who was upset when he entered his cabin. He called the purser. The purser was unable to understand the man due to his accent and loud voice. After he calmed the distraught passenger, the passenger told the purser, "I have paid for an ocean view and I got a parking lot view." Pausing for a moment, the purser said he would resolve the problem within twenty minutes . . . just as soon as the ship left the dock.

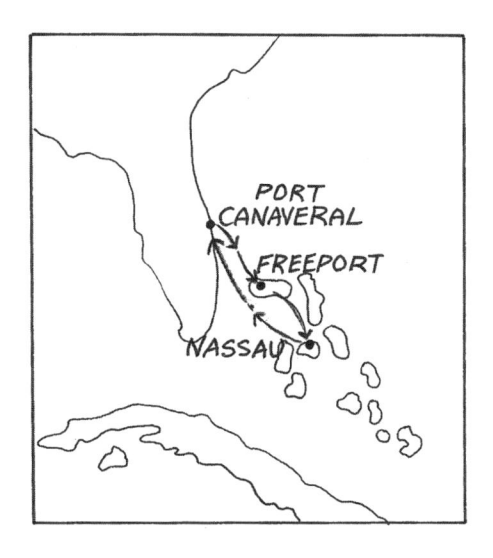

On a rough cruise, one of the passengers got sea sick during dinner. The waiter, seeing the potential disruption of the meals of other passengers, quickly put a napkin over the contents of the plate and removed it. He then escorted the passenger to her cabin. The following morning, the recovered passenger called the dining room looking for her false teeth. Unable to find them, the dining room manager contacted the waiter who indicated he had thrown out the entire contents of the plate. Upon her return to the U.S., the passenger contacted her attorney to file suit. Apparently the suit was settled because her complaint "had no bite."

When booking a cruise, the first question is "where does the ship go?" Make sure you fully understand a cruise may stop at a destination, but it may not let you off the ship unless you purchase some type of shore excursion. In many cases, such as an Alaska trip, the shore trips make the entire experience worthwhile. These are *not* included in the cost of the cruise, the air, or the overnight hotel stay, however. To budget an Alaska cruise, double the total cost provided by the cruise.

On the other hand, a trip from Los Angeles to Catalina and Enscenada has only a few possible tour options. These cruises are normally three or four days and are designed to get away from daily routines. Many of the passengers have sailed before, been drunk before, and lost their shirts before in the casino.

### ✈Travel Tip: Daze versus Nights

Cruise ships are sold by days. For instance, a four-day cruise could depart at 5 P.M. on Monday and return at 7 A.M. on Friday. Using a twenty-four-hour day, you have received three days plus fourteen hours. Hotels sell by the night. You could arrive early, say 10 A.M. (having requested an early check-in) and depart at 3 P.M. the following day (having requested a late check-out) and only pay for one night. In this case, you received a full twenty-four-hour day plus five hours. There is no late check out or early check in on a cruise, although you could be the first person to board and the last person to leave. The cruise does not offer much recreation prior to leaving port, though.

## Chapter 26
### Dr. Travel Prescribes: Cruise Control … for Auto Pilots

Recently our office received a call from the winner of a cruise from Miami to Cozumel. The dilemma facing this passenger was she had a passport from Bolivia and a U.S. green card. She wanted to know about a visa. We informed her the cruise lines, the Mexican Government Tourist Office, and her local U.S. Government passport office could answer her questions. After a moment of deliberation she said, "And what about my Master Card? Do I need to contact them to get permission to use it, as well?"

> *I've learned the most important accessory to pack for an Alaskan cruise is my checkbook.*
> — Jim Feldman

The cruise business is booming. Seasoned travelers, honeymooners, and even entire wedding parties now take cruises. Traditional cruises, eco-voyages, special interests, gourmet, golf, and other specialty cruises make the selection process unending.

Remember to ask these questions:

- ✓ How many passengers are on board?
- ✓ Does the itinerary match my lifestyle?
- ✓ Are families welcome?
- ✓ Are optional activities offered and at what price?
- ✓ Do I have to purchase from the cruise line or can I get the same services on shore?
- ✓ Are there any physical requirements for the tour?

I recently suggested that a client, who is a golf fanatic, take a sixteen-day cruise featuring (what else?) golf outings at twelve courses throughout the British Isles — England, Ireland, Scotland, and Wales — paired with cathedral tours and nature hikes. Remember the only limitation to a cruise is it requires water to sail upon.

"Reach out and meet someone" is the reason most people take cruises. After the cruise leaves port, all passengers are instructed to put on their life vests for a life-saving drill. As each person strug-

## Part IV
## Upon Arrival

gles with the "Mae West," each one starts to laugh and discuss this "life-saving vehicle." Within moments, dates to meet in the bar, have lunch, or get acquainted are being made throughout the ship. Each person is stripped of any pretense, material worth, and the remote chance this could not be a drill the next time the vests are worn. With movies, such as *Titanic*, hitting the big screen, passengers are reminded the ocean is unwavering in its capability to shift from calm to storm and from storm to typhoon. For this reason, the life-vest drill is required by the Coast Guard. But it does become a wonderful icebreaker in every cruise from Alaska to the Virgin Islands. Even though 2,100 people crowd on the decks of a super liner, the cruise is still one of the most well-structured social events of your travel time. When you want to reach out and meet someone, all you have to do is reach out. . . .

> *Never praise the crew on a cruise ship. If you do it too much, they may think you're going overboard.*
> — Karine Armstrong

**Here's a partial list of cruise lines:**

Carnival (owned by Carnival Cruise Lines)
Windstar (owned by Carnival Cruise Lines)
Holland America (owned by Carnival Cruise Lines)
Costa Cruises (owned by Carnival Cruise Lines)
Royal Caribbean International (RCCL)
Celebrity Cruise Lines (owned by RCCL)
Seabourn Cruise Line
Star Clipper
Windjammer Barefoot Cruises
Disney Cruise Line
Cunard Line
Norwegian Cruise

## Chapter 26
### Dr. Travel Prescribes: Cruise Control... for Auto Pilots

*In a* Peanuts® *comic strip . . . 'Life is a cruise ship!' Lucy proclaims to Charlie Brown. Lucy goes on to explain that some people sit in their deck chairs facing the stern of the ship so they can see where they've been, while others face the bow to see where they're going. 'Which way does your deck chair face, Charlie Brown?' Lucy asks. 'I don't know,' answers Charlie Brown. 'I've never been able to get my deck chair open.'*

— Charles Schultz

# 5

# Returning Home

*The stride of passengers off an airplane is always jauntier than the stride on.*
— Tom Clancy

*A man travels the world over in search of what he needs and returns home to find it.*

— George Moore

## Chapter 27
# Home, Sweet Home

"I travel on the road so much," says comedian Rita Rudner, "I fold my toilet paper into a little point (when I get home)."

Just as you need to adjust to life on the road, so must you adjust to being home again. Things are, after all, different — no one pretties up the toilet paper, turns down the bed, or leaves chocolates on the pillow. Home has no extensive menu, room service, or wake-up calls.

Returning home can be a big transition (especially if you were on a pleasure trip and now you must go back to work). Give yourself time for re-entry. Take a walk in the park or have a cup of tea while you sit and read your mail.

In addition to the physical changes of being home again, when you return from a trip, you are not the same person who left. You come back with new experiences, knowledge, and memories of the world.

Sometimes those recollections are sweet; sometimes they are not. But in one way or another, you are richer for them.

Part V
Returning Home

*I miss the vanished airlines whose names described the wonderful destinations to which their planes flew directly: Western, Piedmont, Allegheny, Southern Ozark, North Central. I miss the orderly, regulated days when I knew the airline to call if I wanted to fly from, say, Los Angeles to San Francisco. In that case, the airline was United. Everybody knew this. Flights every hour on the hour. Do you know who flies from Los Angeles to San Francisco today? Delta. (Delta used to mean the Mississippi Delta, for heaven's sake! Delta was how you got to New Orleans.) United still flies to San Francisco, as it happens. Also Continental, USAir, American, America West, Southwest, Northwest, Westair, Pan AM and Alaska Airline, just to list the planes that depart before ten o'clock in the morning.*
— Charles Kuralt

## Epilogue
# Beyond the Blue Horizon

*Airlines are going to ticketless tickets now. They already have roomless seats.*
— Linda Perret

You've arrived home safely, unpacked your bags, and, maybe, you start thinking about your next trip. Chances are, because of the rapidly changing world of airline technology, your future flights will be much different then the one you just took. For example:

- Look for high-capacity, super-jumbo jetliners seating five hundred or more passengers. You'll be dealing with larger crowds, but you'll get lower fares.

- Researchers are working on a triple-decker planes. These planes could have a restaurant, self-service snack area, beds, conference facilities, baby-sitting, and foreign language classes.

- Office in the sky. One carrier is looking at turning cargo space into a conference room. This airplane will have such amenities as monitors for video conferencing, docking stations to plug in laptop computers, laser printers, and video-cassette recorders.

- Entertainment in the air. All seats will have remote control monitors where, among other things, you can make plane, hotel, and car reservations, access stock quotes, or play elec-

Part V
Your New Home

tronic games. The same monitor will enable you to choose from a selection of movies, videos, or live sports events. You'll even be able to order your drink or go shopping. (A far cry from 1961 when TWA showed the first in-flight movie, *By Love Possessed*.)

- Wireless headphones will enable you to move about the cabin and still listen to the movie.

- Smart cards, a card similar to a credit card with a plastic chip embedded in it, will enable you to make reservations and board flights without a ticket or a boarding pass. This card will also contain your frequent flier number and seat preference.

- Ticketless travel. Smart card or not, airlines are looking at ways to get rid of the multilayered paper ticket.

- If you sit in the higher priced sections of the plane, look for fewer First Class and more Business Class seats.

- If you fly with youngsters, look for family-only sections.

- Nothing to do while waiting for your bags? In the future, you will be entertained (or bombarded) by billboard advertising on luggage carousels.

We can only guess what the future of aviation will bring. Certainly Orville and Wilbur Wright had no way of predicting that over 400 million people would be flying in this country annually. Nor could they have had any inkling passengers would be flying while watching a movie, calling their office, or sipping champagne. One thing is certain about the future of flying, though. If you pack your bags with the tips contained in this book, you will be more than ready for take-off.

*I never think of the future. It comes soon enough.*
— Albert Einstein

To send you on your way, I would like to borrow a meditation from the Zen tradition.

Their version:

May all beings be happy.
May all beings be peaceful.
May all beings be free.

My version:

May all your flights be on time.
May all your flying be First Class.
May all your frequent flier miles be tripled.
May the government not tax your frequent flier miles.

Part V
Your New Home

*The best travel books are the ones that go the shortest distances.*
*The best one of all is about a man who stayed where he was the whole time, Robinson Crusoe.*

– Miles Kington

# Resources and Recommended Reading

**Chapter 1:** Common Sense
*Life 101*, by John-Roger and Peter McWilliams
(Prelude Press, 1991)

**Chapter 2:** A Sense of Humor
*Dave Barry's Only Travel Guide You'll Ever Need*
(Ballantine Books, 1991)
*The Healing Power of Humor*, by Allen Klein
(J. P. Tarcher, Inc., 1989)
*When You Look Like Your Passport Photo, It's Time to Go Home*,
by Erma Bombeck (HarperCollins Publishers, 1991)

**Chapter 4:** Choosing a Travel Agent
American Society of Travel Agents (703) 739-2782

**Chapter 5:** Choosing a Flight
Official Airline Guides (OAG) and *Frequent Flyer* newsletter
(1-800) 323-3537

**Chapter 7:** Cheap Travel
*Best Fares* magazine (1-800) 635-3033
*Worldwide Guide to Cheap Airfares* by Michael McColl
(Insider Publications, 1992)

**Chapter 8:** Cheaper Travel
*The Air Courier's Handbook*, by Jennifer Basye
(Big City Books, 1994)

Part V
Your New Home

*The Insider's Guide to Air Courier Bargains*, by Kelly Monaghan
(1-800) 356-9315
*How to Fly for Free*, by Linda Bowman
(Probus Publishing Company, 1991)

**Chapter 10:** Wheels of Fortune
*The Packing Book*, by Judith Gilford (Ten Speed Press, 1994)
Travel Mini Pack mail-order catalog  (914) 429-8281
Magellan Traveler's mail-order catalog (1-800) 962-4943

**Chapter 11:** Special Travel Needs
"New Horizons for the Air Traveler with a Disability"
booklet from Consumer Information Center,
Department 608-Y, Pueblo, CO  81009
Society for the Advancement of Travel for the Handicapped
(212) 447-7284
*Traveling with Children and Enjoying It*, by Arlene Kay Butler
(Globe Perquot Press, 1991)

**Chapter 12:** Get Me to the Airport on Time
*From the Airport to the City* (Houghton Mifflin, 1992)

**Chapter 16:** How to Be Comfortable While Being Confined
*Why Flying Endangers Your Health*, by Farrol S. Kahn
(Aurora Press, 1992)

**Chapter 20:** A Crash Course in Airline Safety
*Fear of flying seminars:*
American Airlines AAir Born Program (1-800) 451-5106
Pegasus Fear of Flying Foundation (1-800) FEAR-NOT
USAir Fearful Flyers Program 412-366-8112
Fearful Flyers Resource Guide 513-871-2746
*Frequent Flier: One Plane, One Passenger*, by Bob Reiss
(Simon & Schuster, 1994)
*Learning to Fly Without Fear*, by Ken Hutchins
(Berkley Books, 1990)
"Crash Course," *People* magazine, 10/20/97; pp. 125-128

## Epilogue
### Dr. Travel Prescribes: Resources & Recommended Reading

**Chapter 21:** Jet Lag: Eat, Wash, or Smell It Away?
*How to Beat Jet Lag,* by Dan Oren et al. (Holt, 1993)
*Jet Smart,* by Diana Fairchild (Flyana Rhyme, Inc., 1992)
*Overcoming Jet Lag,* by Charles Ehret and Lynn Waller (Berkley Publishers, 1987)

**Chapter 23:** Renting a Room
American Bed & Breakfast Association (1-800) 769-2468
Best Fares Travel Club (1-800) 635-3033
Entertainment Publications (1-800) 477-3234
Hotel Reservations Network (1-800) 964-6835
QuikBook (1-800) 789-9887

**Chapter 24:** Son of Travel Broadens
*Eating on the Run,* by Evelyn Tribole (Leisure Press, 1992)
*The Restaurant Companion,* by Hope Warshaw (Surrey Books, 1995)

**Chapter 25:** Keeping in Shape When You're Out of Town
*Inn Shape brochures from:*
Inn Shape Program
Marriott Lodging Communications
Dept. 955.62
Washington, D.C. 20058

Additional Resources:

*Magazines and Newsletters:*
*Condé Nast Traveler* (1-800) 777-0700
*Consumer Reports* Travel Letter (1-800) 234-1970
*InsideFlyer* (1-800) 487-8893
*Travel and Leisure* (1-800) 888-8728

*Books:*
*The Airline Passenger's Guerrilla Handbook,* by George Albert Brown (Blakes Publishing Group, 1989)
*The Business Travel Survival Guide,* by Jack Cummings (John Wiley & Sons, 1991)

Part V
Your New Home

*202 Tips Even the Best Business Travelers May Not Know,*
by Christopher McGinnis (Irwin Professional Publishing, 1994)
*You Can't Afford the Luxury of a Negative Thought,*
by John-Roger and Peter McWilliams, Prelude Press, 1988)
*Travel Answers When You Need Them! Ready Set Go,*
P.O. Box 6415, Shawnee Mission, Kansas
International City Travel Guide Letts of London, N.Y.

*Help:*
Aviation Consumer Action Project (202) 638-4000 (publishes "Fact and Advice for Airline Passengers") Federal Aviation Administration (1-800) 322-7873
U. S. Department of Transportation, Office of Consumer Affairs, (202) 366-2220 (publishes "Fly-Rights" booklet)

*Sources:*
Travelpro Luggage is available from (888) 774-3847 or most luggage stores.
Mulholland Brothers Luggage is available from (888) 774-3847 or luggage shops.

| **Airline Name** | **Web Site** | **Telephone Number** |
|---|---|---|
| Aer Lingus | http://www.aerlingus.ie | 800 223 6537 |
| Aeroflot | http://www.aeroflot.org/e-aero.htm | 800 995 5555 |
| Aeromexico | http://www.wotw.com/aeromexico | 800 237 6639 |
| Air Canada | http://www.aircanada.com | 800 776 3000 |
| Air France | http://www.airfrance.fr | 800 237 2747 |
| AirTran | http://www.airtran.com | 800 825 8538 |
| Air New Zealand | http://www.airnz.com | 800 262 1234 |
| Alaska | http://www.alaska-air.com *Complaints or compliments* | 800 426 0333 206 431 7286 |

# Epilogue
## Dr. Travel Prescribes: Resources & Recommended Reading

| Airline Name | Web Site | Telephone Number |
|---|---|---|
| Alitalia | http://www.alitalia.com | 800 223 5730 |
| Aloha | http://www.alohaair.com | 800 367 5250 |
| America West | http://www.americawest.com<br>*Complaints or compliments* | 800 235 9292<br>800 235 9292 |
| American | http://www.americanair.com<br>*Complaints or compliments* | 800 433 7300<br>817 967 2000 |
| American Trans Air | http://www.ata.com | 800 225 2995 |
| ANA All Nippon | http://www.ana.co.jp/index-e.html | 800 235 9262 |
| Avensa | | 800 428 3672 |
| British Airways | http://www.british-airways.com | 800 247 9297 |
| Canadian | http://www.cdnair.ca<br>*Complaints or compliments* | 800 426 7000<br>403 569 4180 |
| Carnival | | 800 437 2110 |
| Cathay Pacific | http://www.cathay-usa.com | 800 233 2742 |
| CityBird | http://www.citybird.com | 888 248 9247 |
| Continental | http://www.flycontinental.com<br>*Complaints or compliments* | 800 525 0280<br>800 932 2732 |
| Delta | http://www.delta-air.com<br>*Complaints or compliments* | 800 221 1212<br>404 715 1450 |
| Delta Express | | 800 325 5205 |
| El Al | http://www.elal.co.il | 800 223 6700 |
| Finnair | http://www.us.finnair.com | 800 950 5000 |

Part V
Your New Home

| Airline Name | Web Site | Telephone Number |
|---|---|---|
| Frontier | http://www.flyfrontier.con | 800 432 1359 |
| Hawaiian |  | 800 367 5320 |
| Icelandair | http://www. icelandair.is | 800 223 5500 |
| Japan |  | 800 525 3663 |
| KLM | http://www.klm.nl | 800 374 7747 |
| Kiwi | http://www.jetkiwi.com<br>*Complaints or compliments* | 800 538 5494<br>201 645 1133 |
| LTU | http://www.ltu.com |  |
| Lufthansa | http://www.lufthansa.com | 800 645 3880 |
| Mexicana | http://www.mexicana.com | 800 531 7921 |
| Midway |  | 800 446 4392 |
| Midwest Express | http://www.midwestexpress.com<br>*Complaints or compliments* | 800 452 2022<br>414 570 4000 |
| Northwest | http://www.nwa.com<br>*Complaints or compliments* | 800 225 2525<br>612 726 2046 |
| PanAm | http://www.flypanam.com | 800 359 7262 |
| Qantas | http://www.qantas.com | 800 227 4500 |
| Reno | http://www.renoair.com<br>*Complaints or compliments* | 800 736 6247<br>702 686 3835 |
| SAS Scandanavian | http://www.sas.se |  |
| Sebena | http://www.sabena.com | 800 955 2000 |
| Singapore | http://www.singaporeair | 800 742 3333 |
| South African |  | 800 722 9675 |

## Epilogue
### Dr. Travel Prescribes: Resources & Recommended Reading

| Airline Name | Web Site | Telephone Number |
|---|---|---|
| Southwest | http://www.iflyswa.com *Complaints or compliments* | 800 435 9792 214 904 4223 |
| SunJet | | 800 478 6538 |
| Swissai | http://www.swissair.com | 800 221 4750 |
| Thai | | 800 426 5204 |
| Tower | | 800 221 2500 |
| TWA | http://www.twa.com | 800 221 2000 314 589 3600 |
| United | http://www.ual.com *Complaints or compliments* | 800 241 6522 847 700 6796 |
| US Airways | http://www.usairways.com *Complaints or compliments* | 800 428 4322 910 661 0061 |
| Vanguard | | 800 826 4827 |
| Virgin Atlantic | http://www.fly.virgin.com | 800 862 8621 |
| Western Pacific | http://www.westpac.com | 800 930 3030 |

| Hotel Name | Web Site | Telephone Number |
|---|---|---|
| Amerisuites | | 800 833 1516 |
| Aston | | 800 922 7866 |
| Best Western | http://www.bestwestern.com/best.html | 800 528 1234 |
| Budget Hosts | | 800 283 4678 |
| Canadian Pacific | | 800 441 1414 |
| Comfort Inns | | 800 228 5150 |

Part V
Your New Home

| Hotel Name | Web Site | Telephone Number |
|---|---|---|
| Choice Hotels | http://www.hotelchoice.com | |
| Courtyard | | 800 321 2211 |
| Club Hotel by Doubletree | http://www.clubhotels.com | |
| Crowne Plaza | http://www.crowneplaza.com | |
| Crown Sterling | | 800 433 4600 |
| Days Inn | | 800 329 7466 |
| Disney World | | 407-934 7639 |
| Disney Resorts (All) | | http://www.disney.com |
| Doubletree | http://www.doubletreehotels.com | 800 222 8733 |
| Econo Lodge | | 800 424 6423 |
| Embassy Suites | http://www.embassy-suites.com | 800 362 2779 |
| Exel Inns | | 800 356 8013 |
| Fairfield Inn | | 800 228 2800 |
| Fairmont | | 800 527 4727 |
| Forte & Le Meridien | | 800 225 5843 |
| Forte | http://www.forte-hotels.com | |
| Four Seasons | http://www.fshr.com | 800 332 3442 |
| Hawthorn Suites | http://www.hawthorn.com | 800 527 1133 |
| Hilton | http://www.hilton.com | 800 445 8667 |

# Epilogue
## Dr. Travel Prescribes: Resources & Recommended Reading

| Hotel Name | Web Site | Telephone Number |
|---|---|---|
| Hilton International | | 800 445 8667 |
| Holiday Inn | http://www.holiday-inn.com | 800 465 4329 |
| Homewood Suites | http://www.homewood-suites.com | 800 225 5466 |
| Hotel Reservations Network | http://www.180096hotel.com | |
| Howard Johnson | | 800 446 4656 |
| Hyatt | http://www.hyatt.com | 800 233 1234 |
| Inter-Continental | http://www.interconti.com | 800 327 0200 |
| Knights Inns | | 800 843 5644 |
| La Quinta | | 800 531 5900 |
| Loews | http://www.loewshotels.com | 800 235 6397 |
| Marriott | http://www.marriott.com | 800 228 9290 |
| National 9 | | 800 524 9999 |
| Nikko | | 800 645 5687 |
| Omni | http://www.omnihotels.com | 800 843 6664 |
| Outrigger | http://www.outrigger.com | 800 462 6262 |
| Quality Inns | | 800 228 5151 |
| Radisson | http://www.radisson.com | 800 333 3333 |
| Ramada | | 800 722 9467 |
| Red Roof | http://www.redroof.com | 800 843 7663 |

Part V
Your New Home

| Hotel Name | Web Site | Telephone Number |
|---|---|---|
| Renaissance | http://www.renaissancehotels.com | 800 468 3571 |
| Ritz-Carlton | | 800 241 3333 |
| Rodeway Inns | | 800 228 2000 |
| Sheraton | http://www.sheraton.com | 800 325 3535 |
| Super 8 | http://www.super8motels.com/super8.html | 800 800 8000 |
| Travelodge | | 800 578 7878 |
| Westin | http://www.westin.com | 800 228 3000 |

| Cruise Lines | Web Site | Telephone Number |
|---|---|---|
| American Hawaii Cruises | http://www.cruisehawaii.com | |
| Big Red Boat | http://www.bigredboat.com | |
| Carnival | http://www.carnival.com | |
| Celebrity | http://www.celebrity-cruises.com | |
| Cunard | http://www.cunardline.com | |
| Holland America | http://www.hollandamerica.com | |
| Norwegian | http://www.NCL.com | |
| Royal Caribbean | http://www.royalcaribbean.com | |

| Car Rental | Web Site | Telephone Number |
|---|---|---|
| Advantage | | 800 777 5500 |
| Alamo | http://www.goalamolcom | 800 462 5266 |

# Epilogue
## Dr. Travel Prescribes: Resources & Recommended Reading

| Car Rental | Web Site | Telephone Number |
|---|---|---|
| Auto Europe | http://www.autoeurope.com | 800 223 5555 |
| Avis | http://www.avis.com | 800 331 1212 |
| Avis International | | 800 331 1084 |
| Bon Voyage | | 800 272 3299 |
| Budget | http://www.budgetrentacar.com | 800 527 0700 |
| Budget International | | 800 472 3325 |
| Dollar | http://www.dollarcar.com | 800 800 4000 |
| Dollar International | | 800 800 6000 |
| Enterprise | http://www.pickenterprise.com | 800 325 8007 |
| Hertz | http://www.hertz.com | 800 654 3131 |
| Hertz International | | 800 654 3001 |
| Kemwel | http://www.kemwel.com | 800 678 0678 |
| National | http://www.nationalcar.com/index.html | 800 328 4567 |
| National International | | 800 227 3876 |
| Payless | http://www.paylesscar.com | 800 729 5377 |
| Rent A Wreck | | 800 535 1391 |
| The Rental Car Guide | http://www.bnm.com | |
| Thrifty | http://www.thrifty.com | 800 367 2277 |
| Ugly Duckling | | 800 843 3825 |
| Value | | 800 468 2583 |

Part V
Your New Home

| Rail | Web Site | Telephone Number |
|---|---|---|
| Amtrak | HYPERLINK http://www.amtrak.com | |
| Deutsche Bahn | HYPERLINK http://www.bahn.de | |
| Rail Europe | HYPERLINK http://www.raileurope.com | |
| VIA Rail Canada | HYPERLINK http://www.viarail.c | |

| Other Travel Info Sites | Web Site | Telephone Number |
|---|---|---|
| Alabama Bureau of Tourism | http://www.touralabama.org | |
| Albuquerque Convention and Visitors Bureau | http://www.abqcvb.org | |
| American Airlines Training/ Conference Center | HYPERLINK http://www.amrcorp.com | |
| Bermuda Department of Tourism | http://www.bermuda tourism.com | |
| Birmingham (England) Convention Visitor Bureau | birmingham.org.uk | |
| Dept. of Transportaion | http://www.dot.gov/ affairs/index.htm | |
| Greyhound Bus Lines | http://www.greyhound.com | |
| Greater | http://www.bostonusa.com | |

## Epilogue
### Dr. Travel Prescribes: Resources & Recommended Reading

| **Other Travel Info Sites** | **Web Site** | **Telephone Number** |
|---|---|---|
| Boston Convention & Visitors Bureau | | |
| Tourism British Columbia | http://www.tbc.gov.bc.ca | |
| British Virgin Islands Tourist Board | http://www.aip.com/britishvi | |
| TRAVEL Canada | http://www.aip.com/travelcanada | |
| Cancun Convention Center | http://www.globalSites.com | |
| Chicago Convention and Tourism Bureau | http://www.chicago.il.org | |
| Colorado Springs Convention/Visitors Bureau | http://www.coloradosprings-travel.com/cscvb | |
| Curacao Convention Bureau | http://www.curacao-tourism.com | |
| Dallas Convention and Visitors Bureau | cityview.com/dallas | |
| Danish Tourist Board | http://www.visitdenmark.com | |

Part V
Your New Home

| Other Travel Info Sites | Web Site | Telephone Number |
|---|---|---|
| Denver Metro Convention/ Visitors Bureau | http://www.denver.org | |
| Hawaii Visitors Bureau | http://www.visit.hawaii.org | |
| Hong Kong Convention/ Incentive Travel Bureau | http://www.hkta.org/ | |
| Hong Kong Tourist Bureau | http://www.hkta.org/ | |
| Indianapolis Convention/Visitors Authority | http://http://www.indy.org | |
| Health Online | http://www.tripprep.com | |
| Malaysia Tourism Promotion Board | http://www.tourism.gov.my | |
| Maps On Us | http://www.mapsonus.com | |
| Mexican Government Tourism Office | mexico-travel.com/ | |
| Nashville Convention/ Visitors Bureau | nashville.musiccityusa.com/tour | |
| National Park Service | http://www.nps.gov | |
| Newport | http://www.gonewport.com | |

## Epilogue
### Dr. Travel Prescribes: Resources & Recommended Reading

| Other Travel Info Sites | Web Site | Telephone Number |
|---|---|---|
| County Convention/ Visitors Bureau | | |
| Ontario Convention/ Visitors Bureau | http://www.ontariocvb.org | |
| Ottawa Tourism and Convention Authority | HYPERLINK http://www.tourottawa.org | |
| Palm Springs Desert Resorts Convention/ Visitors Bureau | http://www.desert-resorts.com | |
| Phoenix and Valley of the Sun Convention and Visitors Bureau | http://www.arizonaguide.com/phxcvb | |
| Plus (ATMs) | http://www.visa.com/cgi nin/vee/pd/atm/main.html?2+0 | |
| Tourism Quebec | http://www.tourism.qouv.qc.ca | |
| Greater Quebec Area Tourism/ Convention Center | http://www.quebec_region.cuq.qc.ca | |
| Far North Queensland Promotional Bureau | www2.eis.net.au/~nqtds/ \cairns/1fnqpb0.html | |
| Singapore Tourist Promotion Board | http://www.newasia-singapore.com | |

Part V
Your New Home

| **Other Travel Info Sites** | **Web Site** | **Telephone Number** |
|---|---|---|
| Tourism Authority of Thailand | http://www.tat.or.th/ | |
| Metro Toronto Convention/ Visitors Association | http://www.tourism-toronto.com/ | |
| Tourism and Industrial Development Co. of Trinidad and Tobago | http://www.tidco.co.tt | |
| Cirrus (ATMs) | http://www.mastercard.com/atm | |
| U.S. Customs | http://www.customs.ustreas.gov | |
| Vancouver Convention/ Visitors Bureau | http://www.travel.bc.ca/vancouver | |